GĪTĀ-MĀDHURYA

(The Melody Eternal)

Swami Ramsukhdas

Fourth Reprint 2007 2,000
Total 10,000

❖ Price : Rs. 15
(Fifteen Rupees only)

ISBN 81-293-0091-5

Printed & Published by :
Gita Press, Gorakhpur—273005 (INDIA)
(a unit of Gobind Bhavan-Karyalaya, Kolkata)

Phone - (0551) 2334721; Fax - (0551) 2336997
e-mail : **booksales@gitapress.org** website : **www.gitapress.org**

II Śrī Hariḥ II

Preface

The Bhagavadgītā is an indispensable universal sacred book which is a true guide for all human beings. Keeping its utility in view Reverend Svāmījī Śrī Rāmasukhadāsajī Mahārāja has presented this scripture in the form of questions and answers in a very simple language so that the readers may get interested in it and understand it easily. It is also a very useful book for daily reading.

We want to request the readers to study this book themselves and also inspire their close relatives and friends to study it.

Publishers

Gītā

The Melody Eternal

Vasudeva sutaṁ devaṁ kaṁsa cāṇūra mardanam,
Devakī paramānandaṁ kṛṣṇaṁ vande jagadgurum.
Jijñāsāpūrtaye ṭīkā likhitā sādhakasya yā,
Sañjīvanī praveśāya mādhuryaṁ likhyate mayā.

I salute Lord Kṛṣṇa, the teacher of the world, the son of Vasudeva, the destroyer of Kaṁsa and Cāṇūra, the supreme bliss of Devakī.

I have written 'Gītā' the Melody Eternal (Gītā-Mādhurya) to satisfy the curiosity of the strivers and to lead them to 'Reanimating Herb' for strivers (Sādhaka-Sañjīvanī).

Śrī Hariḥ

Contents

INTRODUCTION

After the expiration of twelve years of exile and residing in an unknown place for one year, the Pāṇḍavas demanded half of their kingdom from Duryodhana as was his promise, but he refused to give even as much land as could be covered by the point of a needle, without waging war. The Pāṇḍavas sought permission from their mother Kuntī and accepted the challenge of the war. After this decision both the Kauravas and the Pāṇḍavas began preparation for it.

Sage Vedavyāsa had great affection for Dhṛtarāṣṭra the blind king of Hastināpura. Due to his affection he said to Dhṛtarāṣṭra, "War and massacre of the Kṣatriyas is inevitable. If you want to see the scene of the battlefield, I can endow you with divine insight so as to enable you to see the scene of war from the place you are sitting." Dhṛtarāṣṭra said, "I have been blind all my life. Now I do not want to see the slaughter of my own kith and kin. But I want to hear the details of the war." Then Sage Vyāsa said, "I endow Sañjaya with this divine insight by which he will know, hear and see not only the incidents of the battlefield but also the ideas in the minds of the warriors and will narrate them to you." Saying so Sage Vyāsa endowed Sañjaya with the divine vision.

The battle started on the battlefield of Kurukṣetra at the appointed hour. Sañjaya stayed in the battlefield for ten days. When Bhīṣma being badly wounded with the arrows, fell off the chariot, Sañjaya conveyed the message to Dhṛtarāṣṭra, who at that time was present in Hastināpura. Hearing this news Dhṛtarāṣṭra was filled with sorrow and started weeping. Then he asked Sañjaya to narrate to him all the details of the war. Upto the twenty-fourth chapter of the Bhīṣma Parva (section), Sañjaya narrated the incidents of the war. In the beginning of the twenty-fifth chapter Dhṛtarāṣṭra asks Sañjaya—

Śrī Hariḥ

Chapter I

The Pāṇḍavas spent twelve years in exile and stayed for one year in an unknown place not to be recognised by anyone. After the expiry of this period they demanded half the kingdom as was promised to them earlier. But Duryodhana did not agree to give even as much land as a pin-point without the battle. Therefore the Pāṇḍavas, with the consent of their mother Kuntī, accepted the challenge. Thus both the Kauravas and the Pāṇḍavas decided to fight and started preparations for it.

Sage Vyāsa had great affection for Dhṛtarāṣṭra. So the sage said to him, "The battle and the destruction of Kṣatriyas is inevitable. It can't be avoided. If you want to see the scene of the battle, I can endow you with intuitive vision so that you may see the scene from here." Dhṛtarāṣṭra said, "I have been blind throughout my life. So now I don't want to see the massacre of my family. But I want to have true knowledge of the events of the war-front." Then sage Vyāsa said, "I bestow on Sañjaya this faculty of intuitive knowledge, so that he may know, hear and see all the events of the war-front and relate them to you." Saying so Sage Vyāsa bestowed on Sañjaya this faculty of intuitive knowledge. At that time both the armies were stationed on the war-front of Kurukṣetra to wage the war.

Now the question arises why Lord Kṛṣṇa preached the gospel of the Gītā to Arjuna at the time when both the armies were prepared to wage the war. The answer is that Lord Kṛṣṇa preached him the gospel to do away with his grief.

Under what circumstances was Arjuna grieved?

When Arjuna saw his kinsmen on both the sides and thought that they would be massacred, he was overpowered by infatuation and was grieved.

Why did Arjuna see his kinsmen on both the sides?

Lord Kṛṣṇa placed the chariot between the two armies and told Arjuna to behold the war-minded Kurus. Then Arjuna saw his kinsmen.

Why did Lord Kṛṣṇa tell him to behold the Kurus in both the armies?

He said so because Arjuna had already said, "O Acyuta (one who does not deviate from His divine glory), place my chariot between the two armies so that I may observe the war-minded warriors with whom I have to wage the war."

Why did Arjuna say so?

Arjuna heard the sound of the trumpets, drums and was filled with enthusiasm, so he requested Lord Kṛṣṇa to place the chariot between the two armies.

Why did the conchs blare forth?

When the Field-Marshal Bhīṣma of the Kaurava

army, roaring like a lion, blew his conch, the drums of both the parties blared forth.

Why did Bhīṣma blow his conch?

He blew his conch to please Duryodhana.

Why was Duryodhana displeased?

Duryodhana approaching his preceptor, Droṇa, said, "Behold the army of the sons of Pāṇḍu arrayed for battle against you. You love them, but they have made Dhṛṣṭadyumna the general of their army, who is born to kill you." But Droṇa was not tricked by him and he kept quiet. So Duryodhana was displeased.

Why did Droṇa keep quiet?

Droṇa kept quiet because he understood that Duryodhana was talking in a diplomatic way to instigate him against the Pāṇḍavas. He did not criticize his statement, because it would prove disunity among them, which was not befitting on that occasion. Nor did he support him, because he was playing trick on him and he had no fair dealing. Thus he did not speak.

When did Duryodhana say so and why?

Duryodhana saw the army of the Pāṇḍavas properly arrayed and uttered these words to Droṇa to instigate him against the Pāṇḍavas. It was described by Sañjaya to Dhṛtarāṣṭra.

When did Dhṛtarāṣṭra ask the question?

He asked the question, when he wanted to know the details of the war from the very beginning.

Why did he put the question?

After the tenth day of the battle Sañjaya gave a

surprising news that Bhīṣma, the grandfather of the Kauravas and the Pāṇḍavas, the son of Śāntanu, the chief warrior and the best archer was badly injured and was lying on the bed of arrows. Dhṛtarāṣṭra was shocked and began to lament for him. Then he asked Sañjaya to relate to him all the details of the battle. He said, "O Sañjaya, assembled on the holy field of Kurukṣetra, eager to fight, what did my sons and the sons of Pāṇḍu do?" 1

Sañjaya replied—"Seeing the army of the Pāṇḍavas arrayed properly, Duryodhana went to Droṇācārya and after approaching him he spoke, "Behold, O Master, the mighty army of the sons of Pāṇḍu arrayed for battle by your talented pupil, named Dhṛṣṭadyumna, the son of Drupada." 2-3

Whom should I see in the Pāṇḍava army, Duryodhana?

Here in this army are heroes, equal in military prowess to Bhīma, and mighty archers like Arjuna, such as Sātyaki, Virāṭa, the great chariot-warrior Drupada, Dhṛṣṭaketu, Cekitāna, the valiant king of Kāśi, Purujit, Kuntibhoja and Śaibya, Yudhāmanyu, valiant Uttamaujā, Abhimanyu son of Subhadrā and the five sons of Draupadī—all being great chariot-warriors. 4—6

O Duryodhana, you have mentioned the names of the warriors of the Pāṇḍava army, but who are the warriors of our army?

O, best of the twice-born (dvija), pay attention to all those also who are the principal warriors on our side. You (Droṇācārya), Bhīṣma, Karṇa, Kṛpa, who is ever victorious in battle. Aśvatthāmā, Vikarṇa and Somadatta's son Bhūriśravā. There are also many other heroes equipped with various weapons and missiles, well-trained in warfare who have staked their lives for me. 7—9

O Sañjaya, after telling the names of the chief warriors what did Duryodhana think?

He thought that their army protected by Bhīṣma was easy to conquer, while that of the Pāṇḍavas guarded by Bhīma was unconquerable. 10

What did he do after thinking so, Sañjaya?

After thinking so he said to all the warriors, "Now all of you remain stationed in your respective positions on all fronts and guard Bhīṣma carefully on all sides."* 11

Sañjaya, what did Bhīṣma do after hearing this statement of his protection?

In order to cheer up Duryodhana, Bhīṣma roared terribly like a lion and blew his conch very loudly. 12

What happened after this?

Bhīṣma had blown the conch to cheer up Duryodhana, but the Kaurava army took it as an indication that the war was declared. Therefore the

---

* Duryodhana knew that Droṇa and Bhīṣma were well-wishers of both the armies. So in order to please Droṇa, he first went to Droṇa. Similarly in order to please Bhīṣma, he asked all the warriors to guard Bhīṣma in particular on all sides.

Kaurava army's conchs, kettledrums, tabors, drums and trumpets blared forth all at once and their noise was tumultuous. 13

What happened after it, Sañjaya?

After hearing the noise of their musical instruments, the Pāṇḍava army's musical instruments must have blared forth. But their army did not get any command. Then, seated in a glorious chariot drawn by white horses, Lord Kṛṣṇa as well as Arjuna very loudly blew their celestial conchs—Pāncajanya and Devadatta respectively. After that Bhīma blew his mighty conch Pauṇḍra; Yudhiṣṭhira blew his conch Anantavijaya while Nakula and Sahadeva blew Sughoṣa and Maṇipuṣpaka respectively. 14—16

After that who blew the conchs, Sañjaya?

O King, the king of Kāśī, the excellent archer; Śikhaṇḍī, the great chariot warrior; Dhṛṣṭadyumna; Virāṭa, invincible Sātyaki; king Drupada; the five sons of Draupadī and the mighty-armed Abhimanyu, son of Subhadrā—all these great chariot warriors blew their conchs. 17-18

What was the result of the sound of these conchs?

That terrible sound, echoing through the sky and the earth rent the hearts of the Kauravas, who had usurped the kingdom by foul means. 19

What did the Pāṇḍavas do after the conchs were blown from both the sides?

O King! After the conchs were blown, at the time of the beginning of the war seeing your relatives

(Kauravas) arrayed against him, Arjuna whose ensign badge is Hanumān, took up his bow and spoke the following words to immanent Lord Kṛṣṇa—"O Acyuta (Acyuta—He who does not deviate from his divine nature) (Kṛṣṇa) place my chariot between the two armies." 20-21

Why, Arjuna?

I want to behold these warriors drawn for battle with whom I have to engage myself in this fight and who are the well-wishers of Duryodhana. 22-23

Hearing the words of Arjuna what did Lord Kṛṣṇa do, Sañjaya?

Sañjaya replied—"O King, thus requested by Arjuna—the conqueror of sleep, Lord Kṛṣṇa placed the chariot between the two armies in front of Bhīṣma, Droṇa and all the kings and asked him to behold those Kauravas assembled there. 24-25

What happened then?

Arjuna saw stationed there in both the armies his uncles, grandfathers, teachers, maternal uncles, brothers and cousins, sons and grandsons, friends, father-in-law, well-wishers and kinsmen. Arjuna was then possessed by extreme compassion and felt very sad and said.

What did Arjuna say, Sañjaya?

Arjuna said, "O Kṛṣṇa! At the sight of these kinsmen thus arrayed, longing for war, my limbs, give way, my mouth is parched, my body quivers, my hair stands on end, the bow Gāṇḍīva, slips from my hand, my skin burns all over, my mind is reeling and I am not able even to stand. 26—30

Besides this what do you see, Arjuna?

O Keśava (Kṛṣṇa) I see the omens also inauspicious, nor do I see any good in killing my kith and kin in battle. 31

How will you get kingdom without killing them?

I covet neither victory, nor kingdom, nor pleasure, because what use to us is victory or kingdom or pleasure? 32

Why don't you want victory etc.?

Those, for whose sake we covet kingdom, enjoyments and pleasures, are arrayed here on the battlefield staking their lives and riches. 33

Who are they, Arjuna?

They are teachers, uncles, sons, grand-uncles, maternal-uncles, fathers-in-law, grandsons, brothers-in-law and many other relatives. 34

What will you do, if they are prepared to kill you?

Though they may kill me, I don't want to kill them, O Madhusūdana (the destroyer of the demon named Madhu) even for the sovereignty of the three worlds, how then for the earth? 35

O brother! Don't you want to derive the joy after getting kingdom?

O Janārdana, (He who is adored by devotees for the fulfilment of their desires) what joy can we derive by slaying Dhṛtarāṣṭra's relatives (who are also our relatives)? Sin only will accrue to us by slaying these desperadoes. Therefore O Mādhava, we don't want to kill these kinsmen. How can we, by killing our kinsmen, be happy? 36-37

They are prepared to kill you. Why are you recoiling from the war?

O Sir! These people, with minds blinded by greed, don't perceive the evil of destruction of one's own race and the sin accruing from enmity towards friends. But we, who see clearly the sin involved in the destruction of the family, should at least turn away from this crime. 38-39

What is the result of the destruction of a family?

With the destruction of a family age-long family traditions disappear.

What happens when the age-long family traditions disappear?

When the age-long traditions disappear, sin takes hold of the entire family. 40

What happens when sin takes hold of the entire family?

With the growth of sin, the women of the family become corrupt.

What happens when the women become unchaste?

When they become unchaste, there ensues an intermixture of castes. 41

What happens when there is an intermixture of castes?

Intermixture of castes leads the destroyers of the race as well as the race itself to hell. Deprived of the offerings of lumps of rice and water, the manes of their race also fall. By this intermixture, the age-long caste traditions and family-customs of the destroyers of the race get extinct. 42-43

What happens to the men whose caste-traditions and family-customs get extinct?

O Janārdana (Kṛṣṇa), we have heard that such men have to dwell in hells for an indefinite period of time. 44

When you already know the consequences of the battle, why are you prepared for it?

It is indeed a matter of great surprise and sorrow that goaded by the greed of a kingdom and pleasure we are intent on killing our kinsmen. 45

Now what do you want to do?

I shall be unarmed and unresisting in the battle. In spite of the fact that the sons of Dhṛtarāṣṭra armed with weapons should kill me. That would indeed be better for me. 46

What did Arjuna do after saying so, Sañjaya?

Abandoning his bow and arrows, Arjuna, overwhelmed with sorrow, sat on the seat of his chariot. 47

INTRODUCTION

Duryodhana mentioned the great warriors of the two armies but Droṇācārya did not utter any word. So Duryodhana became sad. Then Bhīṣma blew his conch loudly to cheer Duryodhana. Hearing the sound of his conch, the conchs, drums and cow-horns etc., of the Kaurava army and the Pāṇḍava army blared forth. Afterwards (from the twentieth verse) the dialogue between Lord Kṛṣṇa and Arjuna began.

Arjuna asked Lord Kṛṣṇa to place his chariot between the two armies. The Lord, having placed the chariot between the two armies in front of Bhīṣma and Droṇa asked Arjuna to behold those Kurus. Having seen his kinsmen he was filled with so much of compassion and sadness that he casting away his bow and arrows, sat on the seat of the chariot.

Sañjaya starts the second chapter in order to tell Dhṛtarāṣṭra what Lord Kṛṣṇa said to Arjuna when latter was overwhelmed with grief.

Śrī Hariḥ

Chapter II

O Sañjaya, what was Arjuna's condition when he sat on the seat of his chariot?

Sañjaya said—"O King, Madhusūdana spoke these words to Arjuna who was overwhelmed with compassion and whose eyes were filled with tears of despondency, "How has this infatuation overtaken you at this odd hour? It is shunned by noble souls; neither will it bring heaven, nor fame to you. Don't yield to this unmanliness, because it does not befit you. Therefore cast off this petty faint-heartedness and arise to fight." 1—3

What did Arjuna say, hearing this Sañjaya?

Arjuna said—"O Lord, I am not afraid of death, but I am afraid of slaying Bhīṣma and Droṇa, who are worthy of worship? It is improper to speak even harsh words to them, then how should I fight with arrows against them? 4

O Arjuna, it is your duty to fight. Is it not improper on your part not to fight at such a time?

O Lord Kṛṣṇa, it is better to live on alms in this world than to slay these great-souled masters. I shall enjoy only blood-stained pleasures in the form of wealth and sense enjoyments after killing them. It will not lead me to peace. 5

Then what is the right action according to you?

O God, we don't know what is preferable for us—to fight or not to fight, nor do we know whether we shall win or whether they will conquer us. The greatest factor is how to kill those relatives of Dhṛtarāṣṭra; by killing whom, we don't even wish to live. 6

If you are unable to take the decision, what is its remedy?

O Lord, my nature is weighed down by the vice of faint-heartedness, and my mind is puzzled with regard to duty. I entreat You, say definitely what is good for me, I am your disciple. Instruct me, who have taken refuge in You. But please, don't ask me to fight as You asked before, because even on obtaining undisputed sovereignty on this earth and lordship over the gods, I don't see any remedy to the grief which is drying up my senses. 7-8

What happened after that, Sañjaya?

Sañjaya said—O king, Arjuna—the conqueror of sleep, said to Lord Kṛṣṇa, "I'll not fight" and became silent. 9

What did the Lord say when Arjuna became silent?

Lord Kṛṣṇa, as if smiling, spoke these words to the desponding Arjuna, in the midst of the two armies—"You grieve for those who should not be grieved for, and yet speak words of wisdom but wisemen don't grieve over the dead or living." 10-11

Why don't they grieve, O Lord?

In fact there was never a time when I or you or these kings were non-existent; nor is it that hereafter we shall cease to be. Therefore the wise don't grieve. 12

How should I know this fact?

Just as boyhood, youth and old-age are attributed to the soul through this body, even so it attains another body. So the wise do not get deluded about this. 13

It is right that the body passes through boyhood, youth and old-age, but what to do when we face favourable and unfavourable circumstances such as pleasure and pain?

O Son of Kuntī, the contacts between the senses and their objects, which give rise to pleasure and pain by creating favourable and unfavourable circumstances are transitory and fleeting. Therefore bear them patiently viz., remain equanimous in them. 14

What will happen by bearing them patiently and remaining equanimous in them?

The wise man to whom pain and pleasure are alike and who is not tormented by these contacts becomes eligible for immortality (God-realization). 15

How does he become eligible for immortality?

The real never ceases to be and the unreal has no existence. The seers of truth perceive the reality of both and become immortal. 16

What is that real (imperishable), O Lord?

Know that to be imperishable by which all this world is pervaded. None can bring about the destruction of this indestructible substance. 17

What is the unreal (perishable), O Lord?

All these bodies, pertaining to the imperishable, indefinable and eternal soul, are spoken of as perishable. Therefore do your duty by fighting. 18

In the battlefield there are two activities either killing others or be killed by others. Therefore if the soul is considered the killer or the killed, then what?

Both of them are ignorant, one who knows the soul to be capable of killing and the other who takes it as killed; for the soul neither kills nor is killed. 19

Why is the soul not killed, O Lord?

The soul is neither born nor killed. It is unborn, eternal, everlasting and primeval. It is not killed when the body is slain. 20

What will happen by knowing this?

He who knows this soul to be imperishable, eternal and free from birth and decay, how can he cause anyone to be killed or kill anyone? 21

O Lord, if the soul is not killed, then who is killed?

O brother, it is the body which is killed. As a man, discarding worn-out clothes, puts on new ones, likewise the embodied soul casting off worn-out bodies enters into others that are new. 22

When the soul enters the new body, is there any difference in it?

No, there is no difference because weapons cannot cut it nor can fire burn it; water cannot drench it, nor can wind dry it. 23

Why can't it be cut, burnt, drenched and dried?

It can't be cut, burnt, drenched and dried because it is eternal, omnipresent, immovable, constant and everlasting. This soul is unmanifested, unthinkable and immutable. Therefore, knowing it as such, you should not grieve. 24-25

If we regard it as immutable, there can't be any grief. But if we regard it as mutable, are we not likely to grieve?

If you regard this soul as constantly taking birth and constantly dying, you should not grieve either because one who is born is certain to die and one who has died is sure to be reborn. Therefore you should not lament over the inevitable. 26-27

It is O.K. not to lament for the soul. But it is natural to lament for the body. Why should we not lament for it?

All beings were unmanifested before they were born, and will become unmanifested again, when they are dead. They are manifested only in their intermediate stage. So why to lament? 28

Then why is there lamentation?

There is lamentation because we don't know this fact.

How to know it?

It is not perceived by senses, mind and intellect. So one beholds it as marvellous, another mentions it as marvellous, another hears of it as marvellous. So it can't be known by hearing viz., it is perceived by the self. 29

Then what is the nature of this soul?

O Arjuna, this soul residing in the bodies of all is certainly invulnerable. By knowing this you should not grieve for any being. 30

You have told me not to grieve. But I am afraid of sin. How to do away with it?

Considering your duty (duty of the warrior-class) you should not be afraid, for there is nothing more welcome for a man of a warrior-class than a righteous war. 31

Should a Kṣatriya (a member of the warrior-class) go on fighting?

No. It is only the lucky among the Kṣatriyas who obtain such a warfare that comes unsought as an open gateway to heaven. Such Kṣatriyas are really happy.* 32

* Worldly pleasures do not give real happiness, they are rather sources of pain (5/22). Real happiness is indeed free from pain and it consists in the performance of one's duty. Really happy and lucky are those who discharge their duty sincerely.

What will happen, if I don't take part in such a war that comes unsought?

If you don't wage such a righteous war, then abandoning your duty and losing your reputation, you will incur sin. 33

What will be the result of losing reputation?

O brother, result will be that people will pour undying infamy on you, and infamy brought on a man enjoying popular esteem is worse than death.* 34

Will it also lead to anything else?

Yes, the great chariot-warriors such as Bhīṣma and Droṇa etc., who hold you in high esteem will slight you, thinking that you have fled from the war out of fear. 35

Can I not bear it, O Lord?

No you can't bear it, because your enemies will get an opportunity to take vengeance on you. They disparaging your might, will speak many unbecoming words. What can be more distressing than this? 36

What will happen if I fight?

If you are slain in the battlefield, you will attain heaven. If you gain victory, you will enjoy sovereignty of the earth. Therefore arise with the determination to fight. 37

Will I not incur sin by engaging myself in the battle?

---

* Mere death does not cause infamy, because everyone dies. Infamy is caused by abandoning one's duty.

No. A man incurs sin if he has a selfish motive. Treating alike pleasure and pain, gain and loss, victory and defeat, and thus being even-minded engage yourself in the battle. Thus you will incur no sin. 38

What is additional importance of even-mindedness?

This attitude of even-mindedness has been presented to you from the point of view of Jñānayoga (Sāṅkhyayoga). Now hear the same as presented from the point of view of Karmayoga (the Yoga of selfless action)—

(i) Equipped with this attitude of even-mindedness, you will be able to shake off completely the shackles of Karma.

(ii) In this path there is no loss of effort.

(iii) Nor is there fear of contrary result.

(iv) Even a little practice of this discipline protects one from great fear. 39-40

What is the method to attain the state of even-mindedness, which has been much glorified by you?

In this path the intellect is determinate and one-pointed; whereas the intellects of the undecided (infirm-in-mind) are endless and scattered in many directions. 41

Why is their intellect not determinate and one-pointed?

(i) Those who are obsessed by desires, (ii) who hold the attainment of heaven as the supreme goal (iii) who do actions for fruits as mentioned in the

Vedas (iv) who are deeply attached to worldly pleasures. They utter flowery speech recommending various kinds of acts for the attainment of pleasure and prosperity with rebirth as their fruit. Such people whose minds are attracted by the flowery speech describing pleasures viz., towards pleasures and who are too much attached to pleasures and prosperity can't possess the one-pointed determinate intellect concentrated on God. 42—44

What should I do to escape attachment to pleasure and prosperity?

The Vedas deal with the three Guṇas or modes of Prakṛti and their evolutes in the form of worldly enjoyments. You, transcend the three Guṇas. Be free from the pairs of opposites such as attachment and aversion etc., and be established in the Eternal Existence (God). Don't worry either about the possession of what is not possessed or the preservation of what is already possessed. Depend on God viz., have the aim to attain Him. 45

What will be the result if a person does so?

One, who has obtained enlightenment, has the same use for the Vedas and the scriptures as one has for a small reservoir of water in a place flooded with water on all sides. He does not attach any importance to the worldly pleasures. 46

Is there any method for me to attain such a state?

Yes, Karmayoga is there. In Karmayoga (Discipline

of disinterested action) one's right is to perform one's duty without laying claim to its fruit. One should not be the producer of the fruits of action viz., one should not be attached to one's body, senses, mind and intellect.

Then why should I perform actions?

You should not be attached to inaction too. 47

Then how should I perform actions?

Equanimity in success and failure is Yoga. Therefore O Dhanañjaya (Arjuna) perform actions being fixed in Yoga, relinquishing attachment. 48

What will happen, if I don't perform actions by being fixed in Yoga (equanimity)?

Action with a selfish motive is far inferior to this Yoga in the form of equanimity. So seek refuge in this evenness of mind; for wretched are those who crave for fruit of action viz., they are slaves to the fruit of action. 49

If the result seekers are wretched, who are noble?

Those who are endowed with equanimity, are noble. Endowed with equanimity, one frees oneself from vice and virtue. Therefore, be fixed in equanimity. Skill in actions lies in equanimity. 50

What will be the result of equanimity, O Lord?

Wisemen endowed with equanimity, renouncing the fruit of actions and freed from the shackles of birth, attain the blissful supreme state. 51

When should I think that I have renounced the fruit of action?

When your intellect transcends the mire of delusion, you will grow dispassionate to the pleasures heard and those yet to be heard (enjoyed and unenjoyed). 52

When shall I attain equanimity having become dispassionate?

When your intellect, confused by hearing conflicting statements, has become poised and firmly fixed in equilibrium, you will attain Yoga (equanimity). 53

Arjuna said—"What is the mark of the soul, stable of mind and established equanimity?"

The Blessed Lord said—"When a man abandons all cravings of the mind and is satisfied in the self by the self, he is called a man of stable mind. 54-55

How does the man of stable mind speak?

O brother, his speech instead of an act is in the form of emotion. He whose mind remains unperturbed in sorrows, who does not crave for happiness, who is free from passion, fear and anger, is called stable of mind. Such a man remains unattached everywhere, he is neither delighted nor dejected at meeting with good and evil. His intellect becomes stable viz., his determination for God-realization comes true. 56-57

How does he sit, O Lord?

When like a tortoise, which draws its limbs from all directions, he withdraws his senses from the sense-objects, he becomes stable of mind. 58

How to recognise that one has withdrawn his senses from the sense-objects?

Sense-objects cease for the embodied (soul) who does not enjoy them with his senses, but taste for them persists. This relish also disappears in the case of the man of stable mind, when he attains the Supreme. 59

What is the loss by having this relish (taste)?

O Kuntīnandana (Arjuna), turbulent by nature, the senses even of a wiseman, who is practising self-control, forcibly carry away his mind to the sense-objects. 60

What should be done to do away with this taste?

Having controlled all the senses one should depend on Me and depending on Me, he should be free from all worries. Thus the intellect of the person whose senses are controlled is stable. 61

What will happen if one does not depend on you?

Without depending on Me, one will brood on the objects of senses.

What will happen by brooding on the objects of senses?

By brooding on the objects of senses one will develop attachment for them.

What will be the result of attachment?

From attachment will spring forth desire.

What will be the result of desire?

From unfulfilled desire, anger will sprout forth. 62

What will be the result of anger?

From anger, infatuation (delusion) will arise.

What will be the result of infatuation?

From infatuation there will be confusion of memory. The striver will forget the thoughts and activities of a striver.

What will be the result of confusion of memory?

From confusion of memory there will be the ruin of reason. The person will lose his discrimination.

What will be the result of the ruin of reason?

From ruin of reason one will go to complete ruin. 63

You have told how the man of stable mind sits. Now tell me how he walks?

O brother, his walk instead of being an activitiy, is in the form of an emotion.

The Self-controlled striver free from attraction (likes) and aversion (dislikes), moving among objects with the senses under control, attains placidity of mind. 64

What is the result of placidity of mind?

With placidity of mind, all his sorrows come to an end; and the intellect of such a person of tranquil mind soon becomes firmly established in God. 65

Whose intellect is not firmly established?

He who has not controlled his mind and senses can have no determinate intellect. Without determinate intellect he can't think that he has to do his duty. Such a man can have no peace; and how can there be happiness for one lacking peace? 66

The intellect of the man, who is pleasure seeking (voluptuary) can't be stable. But why the intellect of a striver, who follows spiritual discipline, is not stable?

As the wind carries away a barge on the waters even so of the wandering senses, the one to which the mind is joined, takes away his discrimination. 67

Whose intellect is stable?

O mighty-armed, he whose senses are completely restrained from their objects is stable in intellect.68

What is the difference between an ordinary man whose senses are uncontrolled, and a seer whose senses are under control?

That which is night to all beings, in that state (of Divine Knowledge and Supreme Bliss) the God-realized seer keeps awake; that (the ever changing transient worldly happiness of pleasures and prosperity) in which all beings keep awake, is night to the seer. 69

Does the seer not come across enjoyments?

Yes, he does. As the water of different rivers enter the ocean, which though full on all sides, remains undisturbed; likewise he, in whom all enjoyments merge themselves, unlike the pleasure seekers, attain the supreme peace viz., God-realization. 70

How can the person, who hankers after pleasures, attain peace?

Renunciation can lead him to peace. He who gives up all desires and moves free from attachment, egoism and thirst for enjoyments, attains peace. 71

Being free from attachment and egoism where is such a man established?

Such a man is established in God. This is called the state of Brahmic-Bliss. Having reached this state he overcomes delusion. Being established in the Brahmic state, which is free from attachment and egoism, joy, even at the death-hour, he gets into oneness with Brahma, the Absolute. 72

INTRODUCTION

[The teaching of the Gītā is based on man's experience. While starting this gospel (from 2/11) Lord Kṛṣṇa first of all clarifies that the body and the soul are totally different from each other. The body is transitory, unreal, limited and perishable while the soul is eternal, real, omnipresent and imperishable. Therefore one should neither feel sad at the destruction of the perishable nor should have a desire to maintain the imperishable—this is discrimination. This discrimination is inevitable in all the three disciplines of Action, Knowledge and Devotion. When a man discriminates the self from the body, the desire for salvation is aroused. Not to speak of salvation even the desire for heaven etc., is aroused when a man regards his own self as different from the body. Therefore, the Lord starts His gospel with discrimination.]

This topic of discrimination begins with the eleventh verse of the second chapter and continues upto the thirtieth verse. The Lord instead of using the philosophical terminology has used simple terms to enable the people to understand the topic easily. It means that every person deserves God-realization because the human body has been bestowed upon us only to realize Him. So every human being can realize God by giving due importance to discrimination.

In this topic even the term 'intellect' has not been used by the Lord. In order to distinguish the real from the unreal, the imperishable from the perishable, the eternal from the transitory and the soul (spirit) from the body; there is need only for discrimination rather than intellect, discrimination is beyond intellect. As Prakṛti (Nature) and Puruṣa (Spirit) both are beginningless (Gītā 13/19). So is the discrimination which distinguishes the real from the unreal. This discrimination has been bestowed upon all creatures by God and it is revealed in the intellect. Birds and beasts also know what should or should not be eaten. Even trees and creeping plants feel hot and cold and experience the favourable and the unfavourable circumstances. Human beings are specially endowed with this discrimination which can release them from the bondage of birth and death and lead them to eternal quietude and bliss.

When this discrimination is aroused i.e., when a man can distinguish between the spirit and the body, his affinity for the world including senses, mind and intellect is renounced and his intellect becomes purified and equanimous.

The Lord for the first time has used the term intellect in the thirty-ninth verse of the second chapter where the topic of Discipline of Action begins. He ends with the sentence 'The same ancient Yoga has been imparted to you today by Me' in the third verse of the fourth chapter. In this context the Lord has laid special emphasis on the performance of duty.

In the Discipline of Action the resolute intellect is single (Gītā 2/41). When a man firmly resolves that he has to attain salvation, favourable or unfavourable circumstances cause no obstacle and thus he attains equanimity without making any efforts. When a man resolves to attain God-realization, his attachment and attraction to the world begins to disappear. Attachment to pleasures and prosperity is the main obstacle to the attainment of the resolute intellect (Gītā 2/44).

Having laid emphasis on the resolute intellect in the Discipline of Action, the Lord asks Arjuna specially to perform his duty with equanimity. He declares, "You have a right to action alone but never at all to its fruit" (2/47); "Perform your duty being steadfast in Yoga" (2/48) viz., equanimity. The Lord also declares "Far lower than the Yoga of wisdom is action" (2/49) i.e., action performed for its fruit is far inferior to the Yoga of wisdom (equanimity). He further declares, "Seek thou refuge in wisdom." Then He declares, "Endowed with wisdom (evenness of mind), one casts off during this life both good and evil deeds, therefore devote thyself to Yoga; Yoga is skill in the action." (2/50).

Arjuna had already made up his mind not to fight. So in the thirty-first verse of the first chapter he said, "I do not foresee any good in slaying my kith and kin." Then in the forty-fifth verse he says, "What a great sin have we resolved to commit in striving to slay our own people!" In the fifth verse of the second chapter Arjuna says, "It is better to live by begging than to slay these honoured teachers (elders)." In the third verse of the second chapter Lord Kṛṣṇa ordered Arjuna to arise shaking off this petty faint-heartedness while Arjuna declared his determination not to fight in the ninth verse of the second chapter.

It is a fact that a bearer can't understand what a preacher preaches, if he is already full of prejudices. That is why Arjuna could not have a thorough grasp of the topic explained to him by Lord Kṛṣṇa. He meant to say that an action performed for its fruit was far inferior to the Yoga of wisdom, therefore, a man should perform actions without thinking of their fruit.

Arjuna could not make out the real meaning of Lord Kṛṣṇa's words. They appeared to him to be ambiguous and confusing. So Arjuna puts the question to Lord Kṛṣṇa in the next two verses in order to get his doubt cleared.

Śrī Hariḥ

Chapter III

Arjuna said—"O Janārdana (Kṛṣṇa)! If you consider equanimity superior to action, why then do you urge me to this dreadful action?

Sometimes you ask me to perform action while sometimes you ask me to depend on knowledge. You are putting my mind with the perplexing words. Therefore, tell me definitely the one discipline by which I may get at the Supreme. 1-2

Śrī Bhagavān said—"O sinless Arjuna, in this world two courses of spiritual discipline have been enunciated by Me. In the case of Sāṅkhyayogī, spiritual discipline proceeds along the path of knowledge, whereas in the case of Karmayogī, it proceeds along the path of Action. The result of the two is equanimity." 3

Is it necessary to perform action to attain that equanimity?

Yes, action is necessary, because that equanimity is neither attained without entering upon action nor merely by renunciation of action. 4

Why is it not attained by renunciation of actions?

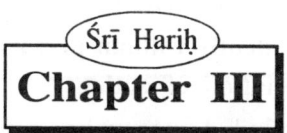

None can ever remain really actionless even for a moment, for everyone is helplessly driven to action by nature-born qualities (modes). Then how can a being renounce actions? 5

If, man sits silently without performing any action, is it not renunciation of actions?

No. The deluded man who outwardly controls the organs of actions, but sits mentally dwelling on object of senses is called a hypocrite and his activity is not renunciation of action. 6

When the equanimity mentioned by You is neither attained without the performance of actions nor by renunciation of actions nor by sitting silently outwardly dwelling on sense-objects. Then how is that equanimity attained?

O Arjuna, the man, who controlling the organs of sense and action by the mind remains unattached and undertakes the Yoga of action, excels viz., he attains equanimity. Therefore, perform your allotted duty, ordained by the scriptures for such action is superior to inaction. And by desisting from action you cannot even maintain your body. 7-8

Shall I not be bound by actions, O Lord?

No. Man is bound by actions other than those which are performed for the sake of sacrifice (Yajña). Therefore perform action (duty), being free from attachment for the sake of sacrifice (duty) alone in order to safeguard the tradition of duty. 9

Why should I perform action at all?

O brother, having created mankind alongwith

the spirit of sacrifice at the beginning of creation, the creator, grandfather Brahmā said to them "By this sacrifice (duty) you propagate and may this yield you the enjoyment you seek!" 10

Why should we make this sacrifice, O grandfather?

Foster the gods through this sacrifice and let the gods foster you. Thus fostering one another disinterestedly, viz., by performing your duty only for others, you will attain the highest good viz., God. 11

What will happen if we don't make the sacrifice, O grandfather?

Fostered by sacrifice, the gods will surely bestow on you the necessities for the performance of your duty without demand. But if you enjoy the gifts bestowed by them without giving them anything in return, you will undoubtedly become a thief. 12

How to escape this sin, O Lord?

O brother, those who perform actions as duty for the welfare of others, as the remains of sacrifice (duty) attain equanimity and are freed from sins, while those who perform actions only for their own comforts commit only sins. 13

O Lord, You have mentioned the ordinance of Brahmā pertaining to duty. What do You say in this connection?

I want to say in this connection that it is very necessary to perform duty to follow the wheel of creation, because all beings are evolved from food; food is produced from rain; rain ensues from sacrifice (Yajña) (duty) and sacrifice is born of action without any interested motive. The Vedas mention the method for the performance of duty and the Vedas proceed from the Imperishable (God); so the Imperishable pervades the sacrifice (Duty). It means that He can be realized by discharging one's duty. So it is very necessary for human beings to discharge their duty. 14-15

What happens if one does not discharge one's duty in order to safeguard the wheel of creation?

He, who does not discharge his duty in order to safeguard the wheel of creation, such a voluptuous and sinful man lives in vain viz., it is better, if he dies. 16

And what happens, if he performs his duty according to your ordinance in order to safeguard the wheel of creation?

Such a man takes delight in the self, is gratified with the self and is contented in the self and for him there is no obligatory duty. For him there is no object to achieve either by the performance of an action in this world; or to loss by the non-performance of an action; nor has he selfish dependence of any kind on anybody. 17-18

Can I also become such a man?

Yes, you can become. Perform your duty well

constantly without attachment; for by performing duty without attachment, man attains the supreme. 19

Has any man performed his duty without attachment and attained the Supreme?

Yes, it is through action (duty) without attachment that Janaka and other wisemen attained the Supreme. Even after attaining the Supreme, they, having an eye to public welfare (by deviating the world from the evil path to the virtuous one) performed action. Therefore you should also perform action keeping in mind the public welfare. 20

How is that public welfare done?

That is done in two ways—by setting an example and by words. Whatever a great man does, is followed by others; whatever standard he sets up by his words, people follow the same. 21

You gave the example of Janaka and other wise men for God-realization. Is there also an example of anyone, who has performed actions for public welfare?

Yes, I am an example. There is nothing in the three worlds for Me to do, nor is there anything worth attaining unattained by Me; yet I am engaged in actions (duty) for public welfare. 22

O Lord, what is the need for You to be engaged in actions?

Yes, there is. Should I not engage in actions, unwearied, at any time, men would follow My path in all matters and so they will not discharge their duty. 23

What will be its result?

The result will be that these worlds will perish and I should be the cause of confusion of castes and of the destruction of people. 24

So for You it is very necessary to perform action. But is it necessary for the wise (enlightened) men also to be engaged in action?

Yes, it is not only necessary, it is very essential. As the unwise perform action earnestly with attachment laying claim to its fruit, so should the wise men act promptly without attachment, for the public welfare. A wise man should not unsettle the minds of ignorant people attached to action, but should get them to perform all their duties, duly performing them himself. 25-26

What is the difference between the actions performed by the unwise and the wise?

The unwise man, whose mind is deluded by egoism, considers himself to be the doer of actions and thus gets attached to them. But the man understands that all actions are being done by the modes of Prakṛti (Nature) and thus the wise man who knows the truth about the spheres of Guṇas (modes) and Karmas (actions)* is not attached to them. 27-28

* The body, senses, mind, intellect, beings and objects etc., viz., the entire world because of being the evolutes of the three modes of goodness, passion and ignorance are included in the sphere of modes while all actions taking place in the world are included in the sphere of actions.

Does a man of perfect knowledge also have as much responsibility as you have?

No, it does not make any difference, if the man of perfect knowledge does not perform action like the man of imperfect knowledge. But the man of perfect knowledge should not at least unsettle the mind of those fools, whose knowledge is imperfect. 29

I get unsettled, my Lord! What should I do?

Surrendering all actions to Me by discriminative intellect freed from hope and feeling of mineness and cured of mental fever, engage in battle (duty). 30

What will happen by surrendering actions to You?

Those men, who, with an uncavilling and devout mind, follow this doctrine of mine, are freed from the binding effect of all actions. 31

What happens if people don't follow the doctrine of Yours?

Those, who finding fault with this doctrine of Mine, don't follow it, know those deluded fools devoid of discrimination to be ruined. 32

How are they ruined by not following your doctrine?

The wise men perform actions in conformity with their pure nature being free from attachment and aversion. But they (the fools) perform actions in conformity with their impure nature having attachment and aversion; therefore scriptural injunctions are of no avail to them and thus they, guided by their impure nature, are ruined. 33

How should a man save himself from this ruin, O Lord?

Attachment and aversion are rooted in all sense-objects. A man should not perform actions under their sway, because they are his enemies. 34

Then what should a man do?

A man should discharge his duty, because one's own duty, though devoid of merit, is preferable to the duty of another well discharged. Even death in the performance of one's own duty brings blessedness, while the duty of another, even though meritorious is full of fear. 35

Arjuna said—When one's own duty is preferable, why does a man commit a sin unwillingly? 36

The Blessed Lord said—It is desire begotten by the Rajoguṇa (mode of passion), anger ensues from it. It is insatiable and grossly wicked; know this to be the enemy which forces one to commit a sin. 37

What is the effect of this sinful desire?

As fire is enveloped by smoke, mirror by dirt and embryo by amnion, so knowledge is enveloped by desire and thus a man commits a sin. This desire, like fire, is insatiable and is an eternal enemy of the wise strivers. It envelops knowledge. 38-39

Wherein does desire abide?

It abides in the senses, the mind and the intellect and deludes the embodied soul by veiling his wisdom through his senses etc. 40

How to subjugate desire?

O noble Arjuna, first controlling the senses, kill this wicked desire, by which Jñāna (knowledge) and Vijñāna (Realization) are veiled. 41

How to translate this method into practice, O Lord?

The senses are said to be superior to the body, the mind is superior to the senses; the intellect is superior to the mind and what is greater than intellect is desire.* Knowing this desire as greater than intellect, restraining the self by the self, slay this enemy in the form of desire which is hard to overcome. 42-43

* Desire resides in the self (agent). So agent is attracted towards objccts etc. The self has two fragments—one is sentient belonging to God and the other is inert belonging to Matter. The fragment of matter is attracted towards matter while the fragment of God is attracted towards God, being of the same class. Therefore desire resides in the inert fragment of the self while in the sentient fragment there resides thirst for divine love or eagerness to know the real etc.

INTRODUCTION

The Lord in the thirty-ninth verse of the second chapter said to Arjuna, "This is the wisdom of Sāṅkhya given to thee, O Arjuna. Now listen to the wisdom of Yoga (Action) i.e., the Discipline of Action in which a person by performing action for the welfare of others without any selfish motive attains equanimity." Then according to the context, in response to Arjuna's question Lord Kṛṣṇa having described the marks of the man of steady wisdom, completes this topic. At the beginning of the third chapter Arjuna asked Lord Kṛṣṇa, "If you think that knowledge is superior to action, why do you urge me to do this savage deed (war)?" In response to his question the Lord from the fourth to the twenty-ninth verses lays emphasis on the performance of actions by which a man attains equanimity. In the thirtieth verse He says that surrendering all actions to Him, with the mind concentrated in the self, free from desire and egoism he should perform actions, relieved from the mental agitation. In the thirty-first and thirty-second verses He declares the sweet fruit of following His preaching (explained in the previous verse) and the harm in not following it. In the thirty-fifth verse He declares, "Better is death in one's own duty." In the thirty-sixth verse Arjuna asks, "By what is a man impelled to commit sin?" The Lord replies, "It is desire, all devouring and most sinful, which is the enemy", and ordered Arjuna to slay this enemy.

Though the Lord's teaching continues from the

thirty-seventh verse, yet in the forty-third verse when the answer to Arjuna's question is over, Sage Vedavyāsa concludes the third chapter and begins the fourth chapter. It shows that the Lord having answered Arjuna's question, gives a pause and then begins again the Discipline of Action which was being described in the forty-seventh and forty-eighth verses of the second chapter by the term 'Imam' (This) in the first verse of the fourth chapter.

There are two important factors pertaining to the Discipline of Action—(1) Performance of actions and (2) Special knowledge about actions. Arjuna wants to renounce the performance of actions. So he says to Lord Kṛṣṇa, "Why do you ask me to be engaged in this savage deed?" Therefore, the Lord lays special emphasis on the performance of duty, specially in the third chapter, while in the fourth chapter He imparts knowledge about actions. He declares, "I shall teach thee such action (thc nature of action and inaction), after knowing which thou shalt be liberated from evil (the wheel of birth and death) (4/16).

This Karmayoga in spite of being beginningless was lost to the world through long lapse of time because of the absence of such scholarly teachers (sages) who could impart it. The Lord in the first three verses describing how Karmayoga was handed down from ancient times, proves how it existed from times immemorial.

Śrī Hariḥ

Chapter IV

You have advised me to slay desire by following the Yoga of Action. What is the succession of that Yoga of Action?

Śrī Bhagavān said—I, first of all, taught this immortal Yoga to Vivasvān (Sun), Vivasvān conveyed it to his son Manu and Manu imparted it to his son, Ikṣvāku. Thus handed down from father to son this Yoga was known to the royal sages. But by great efflux of time, however, it has more or less disappeared. I have told it to you, because you are My devotee and friend; and this secret is supreme indeed. 1—3

Arjuna said—But O Lord! You are of recent origin, while the birth of Vivasvān dates back to remote antiquity. How then, am I to understand that You taught it to Vivasvān at the beginning of creation?

Śrī Bhagavān said—O Parantapa (the scorcher of foes) (Arjuna), this incident has not happened in this birth (incarnation) of Mine. You and I have passed through many births. I know all the incidents and activities of those births (incarnations) while you don't know them. 4-5

Are you not born as I am born?

No brother, though unborn and immortal and also the lord of all beings, I manifest Myself by My own

Māyā (divine potency), subjugating My Prakṛti (Nature). 6

When do you incarnate?

I incarnate whenever there is decline of righteousness and rise of unrighteousness. 7

Why do you incarnate?

For the protection of the virtuous, for the destruction of evil-doers and for establishing righteousness, I incarnate age after age. 8

Is there no bondage for You in taking births (incarnation) again and again?

No, Arjuna, my births and activities are divine. I manifest Myself for the welfare of the world without having any selfish motive. Those who know this fact in reality are not reborn after death but attain Me.9

Is there any proof that such people attain You?

Yes. Completely rid of passion, fear and anger, wholly absorbed only in Me, depending on Me alone purified by the knowledge of the divinity of my activities many have become one with Me. 10

How do they depend on You?

O Pārtha (Son of Pṛthā, Kuntī), in whatever way they approach Me, even so do I seek them. So people get prepared for the welfare of the world by renouncing selfishness and pride. 11

Then why do people, instead of worshipping You, worship the gods?

They attach importance to the worldly things

and seek the fruit of their activities. So they worship the gods; for success born of actions, follows quickly. 12

As men worship the gods for achieving success born of actions quickly, do You also create the world with a purpose?

I create the creatures of the world classifying them into four Varṇas (castes) (social orders) (Brāhmaṇa, Kṣatriya, Vaiśya and Śūdra) according to their Guṇas (modes) and Karma (actions), remaining a non-doer and having no craving for the fruit of action. So I am not bound by actions. Even those who thus know Me in reality are not bound by actions.* 13-14

Having known this, has anyone performed action?

Yes, action was thus (knowing reality about action) performed by the ancient seekers of salvation. Therefore you should also perform action in the same way. 15

What is that action which was performed by the seekers of salvation and which you are ordering me to perform?

Even the wise are at a loss to know, what is action and what is inaction. Therefore I shall tell you the truth about action, by knowing which you will be

---

* God performs actions without craving for the fruit. Similarly we have to perform actions having no craving for their fruit; knowing thus, he who performs actions, is not bound by them.

freed from bondage of the world. This action is divided into three kinds—action, inaction and forbidden action. Truth about the three must be known, for mysterious are the ways of action. 16-17

What is mysterious about the ways of action and inaction?

He who sees inaction in action, and action in inaction, is wise among men and he is a Yogī. 'Seeing inaction in action' means "Perform an action, but do not be attached to it" and 'Seeing action in inaction' means "Be unattached and perform the action." 18

What is that wisdom?

He whose undertakings are all free from desire and thoughts of the world, and whose actions are burnt up by the fire of knowledge, him even the sages call wise viz., this is his wisdom. 19

Where is such a man established?

He is free from attachment to actions and their fruits, has got over the dependence on the world and is ever satisfied. Therefore he does nothing at all, though he may be ever engaged in action. 20

What is the mental make-up of a striver of repose?

He, having subdued his body and mind and having abandoned all objects of enjoyment, has no craving, but he performs sheer bodily action, such a striver is ever free from the binding effect of action. 21

What is the mental make-up of a striver, who has an inclination towards the activity (Pravṛtti)?

He is contented with the available circumstances, is free from jealousy has transcended all pairs of opposites and is balanced in success and failure. Such a striver though acting, is not bound. Not only this but he who is unattached and liberated and who is determined to attain God, and who works for the sake of sacrifice, all actions of that striver melt away viz., turn into inactions. 22-23

What are the kinds of that sacrifice (Yajña), O Lord?

(i) The sacrifice in which all the means, the material, the process and the agent etc., are Brahma, is called Brahma sacrifice.

(ii) The sacrifice in which every material and act is dedicated to Me is called, 'Dedicated Sacrifice.'

(iii) The sacrifice in which the striver identifies himself with Brahma is called 'Identified Sacrifice.'

(iv) The sacrifice in which the striver restrains his senses and deviates them from their objects is called 'Self Control Sacrifice.'

(v) The sacrifice in which the striver's senses function without having any attachment or aversion is called 'Unattached Sense Sacrifice.'

(vi) The sacrifice in which the activities of life-breath, senses and mind are withdrawn and the intellect being aroused, the striver becomes an introvert is called 'Introvert Sacrifice'.

(vii) Utilizing wealth for the public weal is called 'Wealth Sacrifice.'

(viii) Facing difficulties happily, while performing one's duty is called 'Penance Sacrifice.'

(ix) Equanimity in success and failure and unfavourable reward is 'Yoga Sacrifice'.

(x) Study of the sacred books and practising constant remembrance is called 'Knowledge Sacrifice in the form of Self-study.'

(xi) The sacrifice in which the outgoing breath is offered in the incoming, and the incoming into the going, restraining the flow of the outgoing and incoming is called 'Prāṇāyāma (Breath-Control) Sacrifice.'

(xii) The sacrifice in which having regulated the diet the course of both the Prāṇa and Apāna airs is controlled and life-breaths are poured into life-breaths is called 'Special Prāṇāyāma Sacrifice.'

All these sacrifices aim at liberating a man from the bondage of actions. Thus knowing, the sins of the strivers who perform these sacrifices are wiped out. 24—30

What happens when sins are destroyed?

O noble Arjuna, those who offer the above mentioned sacrifices attain eternal God. But to the man, who does not offer sacrifice, even this world is not happy; how then, can the other world be beneficial? 31

Where else have such sacrifices been described?

O scorcher of foes, they have been described in

detail in the Vedas. Know them all to be born of actions; and thus knowing you shall be free from the bondage of actions by performing sacrifice. 32

Which sacrifice is superior, O Lord?

Knowledge sacrifice is superior to the sacrifice born of actions; for all actions and objects without exception culminate in Knowledge. 33

How to attain this knowledge?

Attain this knowledge by prostrating yourself at the feet of the seers of truth by rendering service to them and by questioning them eagerly with reverence. Those wise seers will unfold that Knowledge to you. 34

What will be result of that knowledge?

Acquiring that knowledge you will no more be subjected to delusion and by this knowledge you will see all beings first in your own self and then in me viz., you will perceive the Supreme everywhere.35

Is there also any other glory of this knowledge?

Yes, even if you are the most sinful of all sinners, you will undoubtedly cross over all sins by the raft of knowledge. 36

When we cross the ocean by a raft the ocean still remains. Similarly do sins remain by crossing them?

No, Arjuna, as the blazing fire reduces the fuel to ashes, so does the fire of knowledge reduce all actions to ashes. Therefore, in this human world there is no purifier like knowledge. He who has attained perfection by Yoga of action realizes this knowledge in the self certainly without making any effort. 37-38

How is the knowledge, which is gained by a perfect Karmayogī, gained by other strivers?

The striver who has controlled his senses, is devoted to spiritual practice and is full of faith, attains this knowledge and having attained this knowledge he promptly attains the Supreme Peace. 39

What is the obstacle to attain this knowledge?

He, who himself lacks discrimination and has no faith in others and is possessed by doubt, goes to ruin. The doubting person has happiness neither in this world nor in the world beyond. 40

What happens when doubt is dispelled?

He, who by equanimity has renounced affinity for all actions and by knowledge (about reality of actions) has dispelled all doubts, actions do not bind such a self possessed man.

Therefore, O Arjuna, having cut this ignorance-born doubt of your mind with the sword of knowledge, establish yourself in equanimity and stand up for the fight (performance of duty). 41-42

INTRODUCTION

Lord Kṛṣṇa in the fourth chapter from the thirty-third to the thirty-seventh verse eulogized the tradition of going to the teachers who have realized the Truth, having renounced actions and objects and ordered Arjuna to gain knowledge from them (Gītā 4/34). In this process of Self-Realization it is indispensable to meditate upon God in loneliness. Arjuna did not want to fight because he thought that he would incur sin by fighting. He wanted to attain salvation. So Arjuna thought that the Lord was asking him to gain knowledge by renouncing actions.

Then the Lord in the thirty-eighth verse of the fourth chapter declared, "He who is perfected in Yoga, gains it (knowledge) in the Self." It means that a striver following the Discipline of Action need not go to the great persons who have realized the truth nor has he to practise any other spiritual discipline in order to gain knowledge. Thus Karmayoga (the Discipline of Action) as the means of Self-Realization has been eulogized here.

Arjuna in the thirty-third verse of the fourth chapter heard the glory of the customary method of gaining knowledge and in the thirty-fourth verse by the term 'Viddhi' he held it as the Lord's order for him to gain knowledge by that method. Thus he heard the praise of Karmayoga (the Discipline of Action) in the thirty-eighth verse and the forty-first verse. In the forty-second verse He ordered him to perform his duty of fighting. Thus having heard the glory of 'Jñānayoga' and 'Karmayoga' both and also His order to gain knowledge and perform his duty. Arjuna could not decide which one of the two disciplines was better. Therefore, in order to get his doubt cleared Arjuna puts up the question.

Śrī Hariḥ

Chapter V

Arjuna said—O Kṛṣṇa, You commend renunciation of action viz., 'Sāṅkhyayoga, and the performance of the Yoga (discipline of action). Tell me which of the two is decidedly better? 1

Śrī Bhagavān said—The Yoga of knowledge (Sāṅkhyayoga) (renunciation of actions) and the Yoga of action both lead to the supreme bliss. Of the two the Yoga of Action is superior to the Yoga of knowledge. 2

Why is Yoga of action superior?

The Karmayogī, who neither hates nor desires, should be ever considered a Saṁnyāsī (renouncer); for being free from the pairs of opposites, he is easily set free from worldly-bondage. 3

You said "Both lead to the supreme bliss." Is there no difference in their fruit?

It is the ignorant (children) not the wise, who say that Sāṅkhyayoga and Karmayoga are different. For one, who is firmly established in either, gets the fruit of both. The supreme state reached by the Sāṅkhyayogī is also attained by the Karmayogī. Therefore he, who sees Sāṅkhyayoga and Karmayoga as one, so far as their result goes, really sees. 4-5

When their result is the same, how is then the Yoga of action superior?

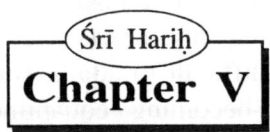

O mighty-armed, without Karmayoga viz., without remaining the same in success and failure, however Sāṅkhyayoga is difficult to attain. But the meditative Karmayogī (by becoming equanimous in success and failure) quickly attains Brahma (Eternal) in the form of equanimity. 6

How does he attain Brahma by Karmayoga?

The Karmayogī, who has subdued his senses and body, whose mind is purified and who has identified his self with the self of all beings, even while acting, remains untainted by actions viz., attains God. 7

How does a Sāṅkhyayogī remain untainted?

The Sāṅkhyayogī by knowing the real and the unreal and being established in the real while seeing, hearing, touching, smelling, eating, going, sleeping, breathing, speaking, passing urine and stool, taking, opening and closing the eyes, believes that he does nothing; the senses are acting on sense-objects. By realizing this fact he remains untainted by actions. 8-9

Besides these two Yogas, is there also any other method to remain untainted?

Yes, there is the discipline of devotion. The devotee, who, by abandoning attachment, offers all actions to God, remains untainted by sins and actions as a lotus leaf by water. 10

A Bhaktiyogī performs actions in order to offer You. So he is not tainted, but O Lord, what is the aim of a Karmayogī while performing an action that he remains untainted?

The Karmayogī, abandoning attachment to senses, body, mind and intellect and also the fruit of action, performs action, for the purification of heart. Therefore a Karmayogī renouncing the desire for the fruit of action, attains the Supreme Peace. But the non-Yogī through desire, is bound being attached to the fruit of action. 11-12

How does a Sāṅkhyayogī perform action, O Lord?

A Sāṅkhyayogī who has controlled his body, senses and mind, having mentally renounced all actions in the body of nine gates (holes), doing nothing himself and getting nothing done by others, remains established in the self. 13

A Saṅkhyayogī neither does anything himself nor does he get it done by others; but does God not determine the doings of beings?

God determines neither the doership nor the doings of human beings nor even their contact with the fruit of actions. But human beings perform action according to their nature and assume doership in it. Thus they have contact with the fruit of action. 14

God does not determine the doership of anyone, but does He not partake of the fruit of actions of beings?

No, the omnipresent Lord does not partake of the virtue or sin of anyone, but knowledge of the self being veiled by ignorance; beings are thereby deluded viz., they assume ownership over action and its consequence. So they are born and they die. 15

Do all beings get deluded by assuming their ownership over action and its consequence?

No, those whose ignorance has been destroyed by knowledge (Discrimination), that knowledge shining like the sun freeing them from the assumption of ownership over actions and its consequences reveals the Supreme in them viz., they realize the supreme. 16

Besides them who attain the supreme?

Those whose mind and intellect are wholly merged in Him, who are established in Him—such strivers depending upon Him, their virtues and sins being wiped out by knowledge, attain God. Then they are not reborn. 17

How do those God-realized great souls behave in practical life?

Those enlightened great souls behold God pervading equally in a Brāhmaṇa endowed with learning and humility, a cow, an elephant, a dog and a pariah. (They don't identify themselves with them in their practical dealings such as eating and drinking etc.) 18

What is the result of their becoming same—sighted in all beings?

Those, whose mind is established in equanimity viz., in God; have conquered the mortal world viz., they have transcended the world. The reason is that the Absolute (Brahma) is flawless and equanimous, hence they are established in the Eternal (Brahma) in the form of equanimity. 19

How to get established in that equanimity?

He, who, with firm understanding and no delusion, neither rejoices on obtaining what is pleasant nor feels perturbed on meeting with the unpleasant, such a knower of Brahma remains established in God. 20

What are the stages to attain that state, O Lord?

He, who remains unattached to external enjoyments realizes the bliss in the self, then he having identified himself with Brahma, enjoys Eternal Bliss. 21

How are sense pleasures shunned by a wise man?

The pleasures which are born of sense-contacts are verily the sources of pain. They have a beginning and an end. Therefore a wise man does not indulge in them. 22

What is the speciality of such a man who does not indulge in these sensual pleasures?

He, who is able to resist the impulses of desire and anger, before he quits the body, is happy and is a Yogī and he is a man viz., he is brave. 23

What happens to such a Yogī?

Such a man free from desire and anger attains the bliss of God. He takes delight in Him and his knowledge ever remains illumined. Such a striver identified with Brahma attains Brahma Who is all peace. 24

Who else attains such Brahma?

Those who have controlled their body, senses, mind and intellect, who are engrossed in the welfare of all beings, whose doubts have been dispelled and whose all sins have been washed away—such wise strivers attain the Beatitude of Brahma. 25

What are the marks of such strivers who have attained the Beatitude of Brahma?

Thcy arc, totally frcc from dcsirc (lust) and anger. They have subdued their mind and realized God. such Sāṅkhyayogīs here and hereafter attain the Beatitude of Brahma. 26

Can this Beatitude of Brahma be attained by any other means?

Yes, it can also be attained by meditation. Shutting out (renouncing) external sense-enjoyments, fixing the gaze between the eyebrows, equalizing the Prāṇa and Apāna breaths (outward and inward breaths) moving in the nostrils; he who has controlled his senses, mind and intellect—such a striver solely pursuing liberation and free from desire, fear and anger, is ever liberated. 27-28

Is there also any other easy means by which all persons may be easily liberated?

Yes, devotion is an easy means. He who firmly assumes Me the Supreme Lord of all the worlds, the disinterested friend of all beings (kind and affectionate without any selfish motive) and the enjoyer of all sacrifices and austerities viz., does not accept himself as the enjoyer, attains the Supreme peace. 29

INTRODUCTION

In the beginning of the fifth chapter Arjuna asked Lord Kṛṣṇa which of the two, the Discipline of Knowledge or Discipline of Disinterested Action, is better. Lord Kṛṣṇa replied, "Both of them lead to supreme bliss but Yoga of action is superior to Yoga of knowledge (5/2)."

Lord Kṛṣṇa described upto the twenty-sixth verse of the fifth chapter how they lead to supreme bliss. Then He described the Discipline of Meditation in two verses which is helpful in the Discipline of Knowledge as well as Action and also leads to supreme bliss independently. Then He concluded the fifth chapter by announcing, "Having known Me the Supreme Lord of all the worlds, My devotee attains peace."

Now Lord Kṛṣṇa in the sixth chapter again explains the superiority of the Discipline of Disinterested Action.

Śrī Hariḥ

Chapter VI

Śrī Bhagavān said—I have told you several facts about Karmayoga (the discipline of action). Now I tell you the essence of Karmayoga. He, who discharges his duty without seeking its fruit viz., without depending on perishable things is a Saṁnyāsī (Sāṅkhyayogī) and a Yogī (Karmayogī). He who has renounced the sacred fire or the action is not a Saṁnyāsī (renouncer) or a Yogī. Therefore, O Arjuna, whatever is called Saṁnyāsa (Sāṅkhyayoga) by people, know that to be Yoga (Karmayoga).

What is glorious in a Saṁnyāsī and a Yogī?

There is glory of renunciation of Saṅkalpa (the thought of the world) for no one who has not given up thought of the world can become a Yogī. 1-2

What is the means which enables a man to become a Yogī?

Action without motive is the means which enables a man to become a Yogī (equanimous). For the same man when he is established in Yoga, tranquillity of mind is said to be the means to attain blessedness (God-Realization) viz., the Yogī should not enjoy the tranquillity which he gets by renouncing the world. 3

What are the marks of a man who has attained Yoga?

Such a Yogī ceases to have any attachment either for the objects of senses or for actions and he renounces all thoughts of the world. 4

What should a man do to attain Yoga?

He should raise himself by his own effort and should not degrade himself; for one's ownself is one's friend and one's ownself is one's enemy. 5

How is his ownself his friend and enemy?

To him who has conquered his lower-self viz., who has not accepted his affinity for the unreal, his ownself is the friend; but to him who has not conquered his lower-self, viz., who has accepted his affinity for the unreal, his ownself acts as the enemy. 6

What will be the outcome if one's ownself is one's friend?

The self controlled person whose mind is perfectly calm in favourable and unfavoured circumstances which he comes across because of his past actions, in present success and failure and in honour and dishonour. Therefore he attains God. 7

What are the marks of the man who has attained God?

His mind is satisfied with Jñāna (knowledge) and Vijñāna (self-realization). His all senses are subdued. He remains unshaken under all circumstances. To him a clod, a stone and a piece of gold are the same. Such a Yogī is called equanimous. He regards well-wishers, friends, neutrals, mediators, the hateful, the relatives, the saints and the sinners alike. Such a man with equanimity stands supreme. 8-9

Is there also any other means besides Karmayoga to attain that state of equanimity?

Yes, meditation is another means. Now I tell you the process one ought to undergo. One having got rid of possessions for pleasures and also desires; having controlled his mind and body; living in seclusion should concentrate his mind on God. 10

What sort of setting should one have for the practice of meditation?

One should firmly fix his seat, neither too high nor too low, in a clean place, with Kuśa-grass, a deerskin and a cloth, one over the other. 11

What should one do after fixing the seat?

Sitting on that seat, controlling the functions of the mind and the senses and concentrating the mind, one should practise meditation for self purification. 12

How should he sit on the seat?

He should keep the trunk (body), head and neck straight and steady, remain firm and gaze at the tip of his nose without looking in other directions. 13

What should be the state of his mind then?

Pledged to the vow of continence and fearlessness, keeping himself perfectly calm, subdued in mind free from the pairs of opposites such as attachment and aversion etc., the vigilant Yogī should think on Me and have Me as the supreme goal. 14

What will be the result of this state?

Keeping himself ever steadfast in this state, the Yogī of subdued mind attains the lasting peace which consists of supreme bliss, which abides in Me. 15

Several persons practise meditation. But why is the Yoga not possible for all of them?

O Arjuna, this Yoga is not possible for him who eats too much, nor for him who does not eat at all; nor for him who sleeps too much, nor for him who is ceaselessly awake. 16

Then who accomplishes this Yoga?

This Yoga is accomplished only by him who is moderate in eating and recreation, temperate in actions, and regulated in sleeping and waking. This Yoga is the destroyer of miseries. 17

When is one said to be established in this Yoga which is the destroyer of miseries?

When the mind, brought under complete control rests in the self alone, and the person has disinclination for all objects without having the least desire for the worldly things, then he is said to be established in Yoga, viz., his Yoga is accomplished. 18

What is the state of mind then?

'As a lamp in a windless place does not flicker'—this is the simile used for the disciplined mind of a Yoga who practises meditation. 19

What is the result of the disciplined mind?

The result is that the mind, disciplined by the

practice of Yoga, comes to rest and he, beholding the self by the self, is satisfied in the self. 20

What happens after he has felt satisfied in the self?

He feels eternal and supreme bliss which transcends the senses, and wherein established the said Yogī never deviates from the self. 21

Why does he not deviate from the self?

He does not deviate because he does not think any gain greater than that and established in that, he is not shaken even by the heaviest affliction; because in that state there is no lack of bliss and no reach of pain. 22

How should this singular bliss be attained?

The state, which is free from the contact of pain viz., in which there is total renunciation of affinity for the world, should be known as Yoga. Such Yoga should be attained with determination with an unwearied mind. 23

Is there, also any other means to attain that Yoga (equanimity as an end)?

Yes, the other means is the meditation on the Absolute (Who is formless and attributeless). Abandoning without reserve all desires arising from thoughts of the world, and fully restraining the senses from all sides by the mind, by intellect full of patience, he should through gradual practice attain tranquillity and having established the mind in God. He should not think of anything else. 24-25

What should he do if the mind wanders away?

He should restrain the wandering and unsteady mind from all those objects after which it runs and should repeatedly concentrate it on God. 26

What will be the result of the concentration of mind on God?

Such a calm minded, sinless Yogī, free from inclinations of Rajoguṇa (the mode of passion) and identified with Brahma will attain excellent (Sāttvika) bliss. 27

What will happen after it?

After it the sinless Yogī constantly engaging himself in God will attain with ease the infinite bliss of oneness with Brahma. 28

What vision about the world does such a Yogī have?

He sees himself in all beings, and all beings in himself. Therefore he becomes even-minded. 29

How does he, who meditates on you endowed with attributes and form, look at the world?

He sees Me in all beings, and sees all beings in Me. Therefore, he never loses sight of Me and I never lose sight of him. 30

Why are you and that Yogī not out of sight of each other?

He established in unity, worships Me as residing in all beings. That Yogī, though engaged in all forms of activities, dwells in Me alone. Thus how can we remain out of sight of each other? 31

How does the Yogī who meditates on you, the attributeless and formless one, behold the world?

He looks on all as one, on the analogy of his ownself, and judges pleasure or pain everywhere by the same standard as he applies to himself. Such a Yogī is regarded as supreme. 32

Arjuna said—O Madhusūdana (destroyer of the demon, Madhu), the Yoga of meditation in order to attain equanimity, which you have taught, owing to restlessness of mind. I don't perceive its stability; for the mind is very unsteady, turbulent, strong and obstinate. Therefore, I consider it as difficult to control as the wind. 33-34

Śrī Bhagavān said—You are right, O mighty-armed—The mind is, without doubt, unsteady and difficult to control. But O Kuntīnandana, it can be controlled by practice and dispassion. This Yoga of meditation is difficult to attain by one whose mind and senses are not under control. But one, who has controlled his senses and mind, can attain this Yoga, such is my conviction. 35-36

Arjuna said—The striver who has faith in the spiritual discipline but whose effort is lax, if he deviates from Yoga at the time of death, having failed to attain perfection in Yoga (God-Realization), what end does he meet with? Without dependence on the world and deluded in the path of God, without any hold, does he not perish like the torn cloud, deprived of both? You can dispel this doubt of mine completely; for none other than yourself can destroy this doubt. 37—39

Śrī Bhagavān said—O Pārtha (Son of Kuntī), there is no fall for him here or hereafter; because, O dear, the doer of good never meets with an evil destiny. 40

What type of destiny does he meet with then?

The striver, who has fallen from Yoga because of having worldly desires, attains the worlds of all the righteous (higher worlds such as heaven etc.), and having lived there for countless years, takes birth in the house of pious and wealthy men in the mortal world. If he has no worldly desire, but falls from Yoga because of any other reason at the time of death, he instead of going to heaven etc., is born in the family of enlightened Yogīs. This kind of birth is very difficult to obtain in this world. 41-42

What happens to him after he has taken birth in the family of enlightened Yogīs?

O Kurunandana! There he regains this Knowledge acquired in his previous birth easily and he strives more than before for perfection. 43

You have told me about him who takes birth in the family of enlightened Yogīs. But what happens to him who takes birth in the house of pious and wealthy men?

He, though subject to the senses, feels drawn towards God by force of his former practice.

What is the force of his former practice, O Lord, by which he is drawn towards God?

O brother, when even the seeker of the Yoga of equanimity transcends the fruit of actions performed with some interested motive as laid down in the Vedas, he who is busy with Yoga but falls from it, is naturally drawn towards God. 44

What happens when he is drawn towards God?

He strives with assiduity, and purified from sins and perfected through many births reaches the supreme Goal, God. 45

What is the glory of such a Yogī who attains the Supreme Goal?

That Yogī is Superior to those ascetics, men of knowledge and workers, who perform action with some interested motive, this is my conviction. Therefore, be Yogī, O Arjuna. 46

Who, among the Yogīs, is the best one?

He is the best one who devoutly worships Me with his mind focussed on Me. 47

INTRODUCTION

Lord Kṛṣṇa in the forty-sixth verse of the sixth chapter described the glory of a Yogī and in the forty-seventh verse He declared, "Of all Yogīs, he who devoutly worships Me with his mind focussed on Me is considered by Me to be the most devout Yogī." When a devotee thinks of God, he gets absorbed in Him. Similarly when something concerning His devotee is discussed, God also gets absorbed in it. In the same state of mind here also Lord Kṛṣṇa full of grace and affection for Arjuna starts the seventh chapter on his own.

Śrī Hariḥ

Chapter VII

Can I also become a Yogī of the best category?

Yes, certainly you can.

How?

Śrī Bhagavān said—With your mind attached to Me and worshipping Me with complete dependence on Me, you will without any doubt know Me in full. I shall unfold to you in full, this knowledge alongwith Realization, having known which nothing else remains to be known in this world. 1-2

Why do all men not know You in reality?

Only a few men have a natural inclination towards spirituality. Among thousands of men scarcely one strives to realize Me, and of those who strive, some rare one, devoting himself exclusively to Me, knows My entire form in reality. 3

What is that entire form?

O mighty-armed! Earth, water, fire, air, ether, mind, reason and ego—these constitute My Prakṛti (nature) eightfold divided. This is My lower (insentient) Prakṛti; but different from it is My higher (sentient) Prakṛti—the life element by which this universe is upheld. All beings evolve from the union of these two.

Who is the origin of these two, O Lord?

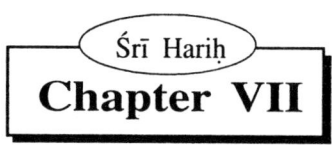

I am the origin of the entire creation, because the whole universe is born of Me and again it dissolves in Me. Therefore there is no other origin in the least besides Me. Like clusters of yarn-beads formed by knots on a thread, the entire universe is threaded on Me. 4—7

How should I know this fact, O Lord?

O Kuntīnandana I am sapidity in water, radiance in the moon and the sun; I am the sacred syllable 'Oṁ' in all the Vedas, sound in ether, manliness in men, pure odour in the earth, brilliance in fire, life in all beings, austerity in ascetics, eternal seed of all beings, intelligence of the intelligent, glory of the glorious and might (free from passion and desire) of the mighty. In beings I am desire, not in conflict with Dharma (virtue or righteousness or scriptural injunction). Not only this but whatever other entities there are born of Sattva (goodness), of Rajas (activity), (Passion) and of Tamas (inertia), (ignorance), know them all as evolved from Me alone. But in reality, however, neither do I exist in them, nor do they exist in Me viz., I am completely untainted and beyond them. 8—12

If it is so, why do all people not know you so?

Deluded by objects evolved from the three modes of Prakṛti (Nature)—Sattva, Rajas and Tamas, the whole worlds does not know me, who am above these modes and imperishable. 13

Then, who know you?

This divine illusion (potency) of Mine, consisting of the three Guṇas (modes of Nature), is extremely difficult to surmount. But those, who having a disinclination for this illusion, take refuge in Me alone, cross over this illusion viz., know Me by My grace. 14

When it is so, why do all people not take refuge in You?

Those who embrace the demoniac nature and whose knowledge (discrimination) is veiled by illusion—out of them the very mean and sinful deluded persons don't take refuge in Me. 15

Then, who take refuge in You, O Lord?

O noble Arjuna, four types of virtuous men—the sufferers, the seekers of wealth, the seekers of knowledge and the men of wisdom worship Me viz., seek refuge in Me. 16

Who stands supreme among these virtuous four?

Of these the wise man, who is possessed of exclusive devotion stands Supreme, because he ever remains merged in Me. So I am extremely dear to the wise and he is extremely dear to me. 17

Are the other three not noble?

All of them are noble.

How is, then, the wise Superior to others?

The wise is verily My ownself—this is my conviction; for steadfast in mind, he is established in Me alone, as the Supreme Goal. The sufferer wants deliverance from distress, the seekers of wealth and Knowledge want wealth and knowledge. But the wise wants nothing. 18

Why does the wise stand foremost?

In the very last of all births viz., in this birth,

the man of wisdom worships Me, realizing that all is God. Rare indeed is that great soul. 19

Why do all the people not worship you thus?

Those whose this wisdom that all is God, has been led astray by desires, constrained by their own nature take refuge in other gods viz., worship other gods, following several methods and rites. 20

Why don't you attract those persons to your worship?

I don't take away their liberty betstowed upon them. But whatever celestial form a devotee seeks to worship with faith, I stabilize the faith in that form and endowed with that faith he worships that deity. But O brother, there is a strange fact that the desired result, which he gets by worshipping that deity, is ordained by Me. But the fruit so gained by the people of meagre intelligence, who worship gods with an interested motive is perishable. Such worshippers of gods, at the most, attain the worlds of gods from where they have to return, whereas My devotees attain me. 21—23

When Your devotees attain You, why is it that all don't seek You?

O brother, men of poor understanding without knowing My noblest imperishable supreme state think of Me, the unmanifest, as an oridnary mortal. So how can they seek Me? 24

They don't know You in Your supreme state, but why are You not manifest to them?

O brother, veiled by My Yogamāyā (divine potency) I am not manifest to them, because these ignorant folk do not recognize Me as the unborn and Imperishable Supreme. 25

Are you not affected by that Yogamāyā (divine potency)?

No, Arjuna, I know the beings of the past, the present and the future. But those deluded by divine potency don't know Me. 26

What is the main reason that they don't know You?

O Arjuna, the main reason is the delusion of pairs of opposites, arising from attachment and aversion. It is because of this delusion that they are subject to birth and death again and again. 27

Are all men deluded by the pairs of opposites?

No. The men of virtuous deeds, whose sins have come to an end, are not deluded. Such men worship Me with a firm resolve in everyway. 28

What is result of the worship with a firm resolve?

They who, having taken refuge in Me alone, strive for deliverance from the cycle of birth and death, know that Brahma (the Infinite), the entire Adhyātma (the totality of embodied souls) and the entire field of Karma (action). They also come to know My Integral Being (that all is God) comprising Adhibhūta (the field of matter), Adhidaiva (Brahmā) and Adhiyajña (the unmanifest Divinity). Not only this but they, with exclusive devotion for Me even at the hour of death, also attain Me. 29-30

INTRODUCTION

Lord Krṣṇa at the end of the seventh chapter while describing His entire form used the six words Brahma, Adhyātma, Karma, Adhibhūta, Adhidaiva and Adhiyajña and explained that the Yogīs who know Him in His entire form attain Him. For getting the clarification of these six words Arjuna at the beginning of the eighth chapter puts seven questions.

Śrī Hariḥ

Chapter VIII

Arjuna said—O Best among men! You have just now told me that your devotees know Brahma (the Infinite), Adhyātma (the embodied soul) and Your Integral Being etc. Therefore I want to ask you "What is Brahma?"

Śrī Bhagavān said—The Supreme Imperishable viz., the attributeless and formless Supreme Soul is Brahma.

What is Adhyātma?

One's own existence is called Adhyātma.

What is Karma (action)?

During the final dissolution all creatures alongwith their actions get absorbed in God. At the beginning of the new creation He reveals them so that they may reap the fruit of their actions. This feat of God which brings forth the existence of being is Karma.

What is said to be Adhibhūta?

O noble Arjuna, all perishable objects are Adhibhūta.

What is termed as Adhidaiva?

Puruṣa (Brahmā) who is the first to appear at the beginning of the creation is Adhidaiva.

Who is Adhiyajña in this body?

I alone dwelling as the inner witness, am Adhiyajña in this body.

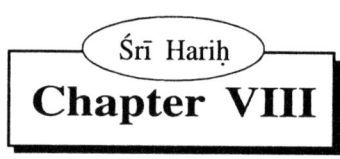

How are You attained at the time of death by those who have controlled their mind?

He who departs from the body, thinking of Me alone at the time of death, attains My being, there is no doubt about it—this is my ordinance. 1—5

What becomes of those who don't think of You?

O Kuntīnandana (Arjuna) thinking of whatever being, one leaves the body at the time of death, that alone he attains, being absorbed in the thought thereof. 6

What is it that I should do at the time of death to think of You?

You should think of Me at all times and perform your duty, with mind and reason surrendered to Me.

What will be its results?

You will surely attain Me. 7

What is Your Form by thinking which a self-controlled man attains You?

There are three forms—one with attributes and formless, second attributeless and formless and third endowed with attributes and form. Now I tell you the first form by meditating on which a man attains Me.

O Pārtha, he who with his mind established in Yoga in the form of practice of meditation, thinking of nothing else, is constantly engaged in contemplation of the Supreme Divine Puruṣa (God) attains Him. 8

What is the form of that Supreme Divine Puruṣa?

He is the Omniscient, the Ancient, the Ruler of all, Subtler than the Subtle, the Sustainer of all, possessing a form beyond comprehension, shining like the Sun and beyond the darkness of ignorance. He who meditates on this Supreme Puruṣa at the time of death, by Yogic power firmly holding the life-breath in the space between the eyebrows, with a steady mind, full of devotion, reaches verily that Supreme-Divine-Puruṣa. 9-10

How can a man attain You who are with attributes and formless by thinking of You?

I shall speak to you in brief the method how to attain the Supreme Goal (God) which knowers of the Vedas call the imperishable, and into which enter the recluses free from attachment, and desiring which the celibates practise celibacy. Having restrained all the media of perception, fixing the mind in the heart, fixing the life-breath in the head and remaining steadfast in yogic concentration on God, the striver who departs leaving the body, reciting the one syllabled Brahma, Oṁ and dwelling on Me in My absolute aspect, attains the Supreme Goal. 11—13

Now tell me—how can a self-controlled man attain You by thinking of Your Form endowed with attributes and Form?

O Pārtha, he who always and constantly thinks of Me with undivided mind, to that Yogī, always absorbed in Me, I am easily attainable. 14

What happens to the great souls who have attained You?

The great souls having attained Me, are no more subject to rebirth which is transitory and the abode of pain. 15

Who are subject to rebirth?

All the worlds including that of Brahmā are subject to return (rebirth), but on attaining Me there is no rebirth. 16

Why are all the worlds subject to return (rebirth)?

Because they are under the sway of time.

What is that sway of Time?

Those who know that the day of Brahmā lasts a thousand Yugas (ages)* and his night lasts a thousand Yugas, know the reality about Time. At the commencement of Brahmā's day (when Brahmā awakes) all cmbodied beings emanate from the unmanifest (i.e., Brahmā's subtle body) and at the commencement of his night (when Brahmā goes sleep) they merge in the same subtle body, which is called the unmanifest. 17-18

Why are they born and dissolved again and again?

The multitude of beings is ever the same. But because of their nature full of attachment and aversion they are born again and again from Brahmā under compulsion at the time of cosmic day and are dissolved in him at the approach of cosmic night. 19

* A Yuga (age) comprises forty-three lacs and twenty thousand years.

Is there any existence beyond the Unmanifest (i.e., Brahmā's subtle body) which does not perish?

Yes, beyond Brahmā there is Unmanifest Eternal Existence, the Supreme Divine Person who does not perish even when all beings perish. He is called the Unmanifest, the Imperishable, the Supreme Goal. That is My Supreme Abode, attaining which man does not return. 20-21

What is the way to attain that Supreme Abode?

O Pārtha! That Supreme Puruṣa, in Whom all beings dwell and by whom whole the world is pervaded, is attainable only by exclusive devotion. 22

What happens to those who have exclusive devotion and to those who don't have?

O Arjuna! Those who have exclusive devotion do not return. But those who don't have exclusive devotion return. Now I shall tell you the time (Path) when they do not return and the time (Path) when they return. 23

Which are the two paths, O Lord?

The path in which are located the fire-god, and the gods presiding over—day time, the bright fortnight and the six months of the northward course of the Sun, proceeding along it after death, the knowers of Brahma attain Brahma viz., they do not return. But the path in which are located the gods presiding over—smoke, night, the dark fortnight and the six months of the southward course of the Sun, the beings devoted to action with a motive, proceeding along it after death, after enjoying the fruit of meritorious deeds in heaven, return. 24-25

How old are these two paths?

These two paths, the bright and the dark are considered to be eternal, proceeding by one (bright), a man has no return and proceeding by the other (dark), he returns. 26

How to check this return, O Lord?

O Pārtha! By knowing the secret of these two paths, no Yogī gets deluded, in the world. Therefore, O Arjuna ever remain established in Yoga viz., ever remain untainted in the world.

What happens when one gets established in Yoga, O Lord?

The Yogī knowing this secret, transcends thc rcwards of mcritorious deeds of the study of the Vedas, and of the performance of sacrifices, austerities and charities and attains the Supreme Primeval Abode. 28

INTRODUCTION

In the seventh chapter Lord Kṛṣṇa was unfolding to Arjuna Knowledge (Wisdom) with Realization (real knowledge of manifest Divinity). But in between Arjuna at the beginning of the eighth chapter put seven questions, So Lord Kṛṣṇa by answering the first six questions in brief answered in detail the seventh question—"How are you to be known at the time of death by the self-controlled?" Now the Lord starts the same topic of Knowledge with Realization in the ninth chapter.

Śrī Hariḥ

Chapter IX

I have listened to what You said in response to my question. But what did You yourself want to say, O Lord?

Śrī Bhagavān said—O brother, I was unfolding to you the most profound Knowledge combined with Realization. I shall declare you (as you) don't cavil again the same, by knowing which you will be released from the evil of worldly existence viz., birth and death. 1

Is that profound knowledge combined with Realization, very difficult to practise?

No, brother, this is the sovereign science, the sovereign secret, supremely holy, excellent, directly enjoyable, attended with virtue and imperishable and also very easy to practise. 2

Why do all people not know this easy sovereign science?

They do not know it because they have no faith in it, so they instead of attaining Me revolve in the path of the mortal world, viz., they are subject to birth and death again and again. 3

What is that profound knowledge combined with Realization?

All this universe is permeated by Me in My

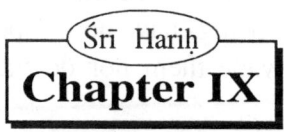

unmanifest aspect and all beings abide in Me, but if it is assumed that beings have no independent existence then I don't pervade them nor do they abide in Me viz., I am all. 4

Who is the creator and base of this world?

O brother! it is I, who is the base, creator and sustainer of all beings. But behold My divine Yoga, that inspite of being the creator and sustainer of all beings, Myself does not dwell in them, I remain totally untainted. 5

Then how do all beings abide in You?

Just as the extensive and all pervading air (which is born of ether) always remains in ether; likewise all beings (sprung as they are from Me) abide in Me. 6

Are those beings liberated then?

No, Kuntīnandana, all beings merge in My Prakṛti at the end of Final dissolution and I bring them forth again at the beginning of the new creation. 7

How long do you continue to bring them forth?

So long as they are subject to the influence of their nature, laying hold of My Prakṛti, I bring them forth again and again. 8

When you bring them forth again and again, do these actions not bind You, O Lord?

No, I remain unattached and indifferent to those actions like one unconcerned. So those actions do not bind Me. 9

Then how do you bring forth the creation?

In fact with Me as the supervisor, Prakṛti brings forth the whole creation, both animate and inanimate. O Arjuna, under my supervision the world undergoes various changes. 10

When everything in the region of Prakṛti is going on by your power, why do people not have faith in You?

The fools, not knowing My Supreme nature as the great Lord of creation, take Me to be an ordinary mortal and so disregard Me. 11

What type of people are those fools, O Lord?

Those fools emrbrace a nature which is fiendish, demoniacal and delusive and they have vain hopes, futile actions and fruitless knowledge viz., they don't bear real fruit. 12

Then who are devoted to you, O Lord?

O Arjuna, great souls, embracing divine nature, knowing Me as the prime cause of creation and imperishable, worship Me with undivided mind. 13

What are the marks of those great souls who worship You with undivided mind?

They constantly chant My names and glories and strive to attain Me, they prostrating before Me worship Me with devotion. 14

Is there also any other way to worship You, O Lord?

Yes, there is. Some strivers worship Me through

their offering of knowledge in My Absolute aspect as their ownself, while other strivers worship Me in My Universal Form in many ways, thinking Me (Lord) different from them (devotees). 15

How is the worship of the universe your own worship, O Lord?

I am Vedic ritual, I am sacrifice, I am offering to the departed. I am medicinal herb, I am sacred formula, I am clarified butter, I am fire, I am the act of offering oblations into fire. I am the sustainer and ruler of this universe, its father, mother and of grandfather; I am the knowable, the purifier, the sacred syllable 'Oṁ' and the three Vedas—Ṛk, Sāma, Yajuṣ. I am the father, sustainer, mother, grandfather, supreme goal, supporter, Lord, witness, abode, refuge, disinteresed friend, origin, end, treasure-house and the imperishable seed of the entire universe. I radiate heat as the sun, I withhold and send forth rain, I am immortality as well as death and also I am being and non-being (sentient and insentient). 16—19

When you are all-in-all in your Universal Form, why do people worship the gods?

They want to enjoy pleasures. So they perform action with some interested motive as laid down in the three Vedas and drink the sap of Soma plant, thus purified from sin, which is in an obstacle to heaven, worshipping Indra, the lord of the gods through sacrifices, seek access to heaven. They attain paradise as a result of their good deeds. Having enjoyed the vast world of heaven, they return to the world of mortals on the exhaustion of their merits. Thus taking recourse to action with interested motive enjoined by the three Vedas they repeatedly come and go (viz., are born and dissolved). 20-21

But what about those who, having no desire, worship You with undivided devotion?

To these devotees, who worship Me alone constantly, thinking of no one else, I supply what is not already possessed and preserve what is already possessed. 22

If anyone endowed with faith, worship other gods, is that also Your worship?

Even those devotees, who endowed with faith worship other gods, too worship Me alone (because I am all being and non-being); but their worship is not in accordance with rules. 23

When they too worship You alone, why is their worship not in accordance with rules?

I am the enjoyer and the Lord of all the sacrifices, gifts, penances and actions. But they don't know Me in reality, hence they fall. 24

What is their fall?

Those who worship the gods, go to the gods; those who worship the manes, reach the manes; those who adore the spirits, reach the spirits and those who worship Me, attain Me alone. So My worshippers don't fall. (They are not subject to birth and death). 25

Is an access to you by devotion very difficult?

No, it is very easy. Whosoever offers Me with devotion, a leaf, a flower, a fruit or even water, I appear in person before that devout devotee and delightfully partake of that article offered by him.26

What should I do?

O Arjuna, whatever you do, whatever you eat, whatever you offer as oblation to the sacred fire, whatever you bestow as a gift, whatever you do by way of penance, offer it all to Me. 27

What is the good that will accrue from surrendering every action to You?

O brother, you will be free from the bondage of action yielding good and bad results and freed from them you shall attain Me. 28

You free those, who surrender every action to You, from bondage. It means that You are partial to them. But those who don't surrender themselves to You, they remain in bondage. Why this partiality?

O brother, this is not partiality, I am equally present in all beings. There is none hateful, none dear to Me. But those who devoutly worship Me, abide in Me, I also abide in them specially. 29

Can a man of sinful conduct worship you and be your devotee?

Yes, certainly. Even if a man of the most sinful conduct worships Me with exclusive devotion, he should be considered a saint; for he has rightly resolved. 30

Should he be considered only a saint?

No, soon he becomes virtuous (very sacred) and obtains lasting peace. O Arjuna, take an oath that My devotee never falls. 31

Can other people also be your devotee?

Yes, Arjuna, womenfolk, Vaiśyas (members of the trading class), Śūdras (those belonging to the labouring class) and even those who are born of the womb of sin, taking refuge in Me, attain Me. What wonder then, that the holy Brāhmaṇas and Kṣatriyas be devoted to Me.

How should I become such a devotee, O Lord?

Having obtained this transient and joyless life, worship Me. 32-33

How should I worship you?

Fix your mind on Me; be devoted to Me; adore Me; bow down to Me; thus uniting yourself to me and entirely depending on Me, you shall attain Me. 34

INTRODUCTION

Lord Kṛṣṇa was explaining knowledge with realization in the seventh chapter. But Arjuna put some questions in between. So the Lord answered his questions and then again started the same previous topic in the ninth chapter and concluded the chapter by dependence on the Lord. But He was not satisfied with what He had already said to Arjuna. As a devotee wants to know His glories in detail (Gītā 10/8), He also wanted to say something confidential to His loving devotee, Arjuna. So by His grace He starts the topic in the tenth chapter.

Śrī Hariḥ

Chapter X

Śrī Bhagavān said—Arjuna, listen to my supreme word* which I shall speak to you with a desire for your welfare because you love Me very much. 1

O Lord, what is Your Supreme Word?

The world has been created by Me, neither gods nor great sages know this secret, for I am the prime cause in all respects of gods as well as the sages. 2

When even gods and great sages don't know You, the prime cause of the whole creation, how will an ordinary aspirant know You and attain You?

He who knows (assumes firmly) Me in reality as unborn and beginningless and as the Supreme Lord of the universe, is a man of knowledge and he is purged of all sins. 3

How should I understand your supreme word, O Lord?

Discrimination, wisdom, non-delusion, forgiveness, truth, control over senses and mind; joy and sorrow; birth and death, fear and fearlessness, non-violence, equanimity, contentment, austerity, charity, fame and illfame—these diverse feelings of creatures emanate from Me. Not only these feelings but the seven great seers and more ancient four Sanakas and fourteen

---

* The supreme word of the Lord is that he is the prime cause of everyone and everything.

Manus (progenitors of mankind), who are all devoted to Me, are born of My will viz., I am their originator and teacher. 4—6

What do you mean when You say that discrimination, wisdom and sages etc., emanate from You?

He who assumes this supreme glory and supernatural power of mine firmly with faith gets established in Me through unfaltering devotion, there is no doubt in it. 7

What is this firm assumption?

I am the origin of all creation; everything in the world moves because of Me. Assuming this firmly, the wise, full of devotion and faith worship Me. 8

What is the method of their worship, O Lord?

With their mind fixed on Me, with their lives surrendered to Me, enlightening one another about My greatness and speaking of Me, they ever remain contented and have devotion for Me. 9

How do you respond to their devotional activities?

To those who are ever devout and worship Me with love, I confer that Yoga of wisdom (equanimity) by which they attain Me. 10

Do you also confer anything else on them?

Yes, in order to shower My grace on them, I, dwelling in their hearts, dispel the darkness born of ignorance by the luminous lamp of wisdom. 11

Arjuna said—O Lord, after hearing Your super human and unparalleled grace for devotees I am very much delighted. You are the Supreme Eternal, the Supreme Abode, the Supreme Purifier, the Eternal Divine Person, the Prime Deity, the Unborn and the Omnipresent. All the seers; the celestial sage, Nārada, the sages—Asita, Devala and Vyāsa have thus acclaimed You; and you yourself also proclaim this to me. 12-13

O Arjuna, do you believe as true all that I tell you?

Yes, Keśava, I hold as true, all that You say to me. O Lord! Neither gods with their divine power nor demons with their conjuring power know your manifestation? 14

Then who knows My manifestation?

O Creator of beings, O Ruler of creatures, O God of gods, O Lord of the universe, O Supreme Person, You alone know Yourself. Therefore You alone can describe in full Your divine glories, by which You stand pervading the entire world. 15-16

Why do you want Me to describe My divine glories?

O Master of Yoga, how may I know You by constant meditation? And O Lord, in what various aspects are You to be thought of by me? Therefore, O Lord Kṛṣṇa, tell me once more, in details your power of Yoga and your glory; for I am not satiated with hearing yours nectarean words. 17-18

Śrī Bhagavān said—Very well! I shall tell you My divine glories in brief; for O noble Arjuna, there is no end to the details of My glories. 19

Which are your divine glories, O Lord?

I am the Self seated in the hearts of all beings. I am the beginning, the middle and also the end of all beings. I am Viṣṇu (Vāmana) among the twelve sons of Aditi and the bright-rayed Sun among the luminaries; I am Marīci glory among the Maruts (wind-gods) and the Moon among stars. Among the Vedas I am the Sāmaveda; among the gods, I am Indra; among the senses, I am the mind and I am consciousness among living beings. Among the eleven Rudras (gods of destruction), I am Śaṅkara; among the Yakṣas (Genies) and Rākṣasas (Demons), I am Kubera (the god of riches). Among the eight Vasus I am Pāvaka (the god of fire) and among mountains I am Meru. Among priests, know Me to be their chief, Bṛhaspati. Among generals I am Skanda; and of seats of water, I am the ocean. Among the great seers I am Bhṛgu; among the words I am mono syllable 'Oṁ' among Yajñas (sacrifices) I am 'Japa'-Yajña (chanting the name of the Lord) and among the immovable I am the Himālaya. Among all trees I am Aśvattha (the holy Pīpala tree); among the celestial sages, Nārada; among the Gandharvas (celestial songsters), Citraratha; among the Siddhas (the perfected souls), the Sage Kapila. Among horses know me to be Uccaiḥśravā begotten of the churning of the ocean alongwith nectar; among lordly elephants, Airāvata (Indra's elephant); and among men, the king. 20—27

What are your other divine glories, O Lord?

Among weapons I am the thunderbolt; among

cows I am the celestial cow Kāmadhenu; I am Kandarpa (Kāmadeva) among progenitors; and among serpents, I am Vāsuki; Among Nāgas (a special class of serpents), I am Ananta; among water deities I am Varuṇa; among the manes I am Aryamā; and among rulers, I am Yama (the god of death). Among the demons, I am Prahlāda; among reckoners I am Time; among beasts, I am the lion; and among birds, Garuḍa (the Vehicle of Viṣṇu). Among purifiers, I am the wind; among wielders of weapons, I am Rāma; among fishes I am the crocodile; and among rivers I am the Ganges. 28—31

O Lord, does your glory also reveal itself elsewhere?

Yes, O Arjuna I am the beginning, the middle and the end of all creations; of sciences, I am the science of the soul (metaphysics); of those who debate, I am the right type of reasoning; of letters I am 'A' (the first letter of the alphabet); of word-compounds in grammar, I am the dual (Dvandva); I am Verily the endless time (the devourer of time); I am the sustainer of all, having My face on all sides. 32-33

O Lord, will You also tell your other manifestations?

I am the all devouring Death, and also the source of future beings; of women I am goddesses presiding over fame, prosperity, speech, memory, intelligence, constancy and forgiveness, of the Sāma hymns, I am Bṛhat-Sāma; of Vedic Verses, I am Gāyatrī; of the twelve months of the Hindu calendar, I am Mārgaśīrṣa; among seasons, the flowery spring. I am gambling of the fraudulent; glory of the glorious;

victory of the victorious; resolution of the resolute and goodness of the good. 34—36

O Lord, what are Your other manifestations?

Among the members of the Vṛṣṇi class I am Vāsudeva (Kṛṣṇa); among the Pāṇḍavas, Dhanañjaya (you); among the sages, Vyāsa; among thc wise, I am sage Śukra; I am the ruling power in rulers; righteousness in those who aspire for victory; of secrets I am the custodian in the shape of silence and I am the wisdom of the wise. Not only this, I am the seed of all beings, for there is no creature, animate or inanimate which exists without Me viz., I exist in all of them.

37—39

O Lord, have you exhausted the account of your divine glories?

No, O scorcher of foes, there is no end of my divine glories. This is only a brief description of the extent of My glories because I can't describe them fully. 40

O Lord, how should I know Your manifestations?

Every such creature as is glorious, brilliant or powerful, know that to be a manifestation of a spark of My splendour. O brother Arjuna, what will you gain by knowing all this in detail? It is sufficient to say that I, in spite of supporting the entire universe with a single fragment of Myself, am sitting with a whip and bridle in My hands before you to obey you. 41-42

INTRODUCTION

At the end of tenth chapter Lord Kṛṣṇa graciously said to Arjuna, "I hold countless universes in fragment of My body and yet I am sitting before you as a chariot driver with horses' bridle and a whip in my hands and carrying out your order. I am the base of all the divine glories and influence (Yoga) and when I am sitting before you, what need is there for you to have the detailed knowledge of My divine glories?" After listening to the statement of Lord Kṛṣṇa Arjuna thinks of His special grace and being wonderstruck speaks—

Śrī Hariḥ

Chapter XI

Arjuna said—O Lord, by the most secret words of spiritual wisdom (I am the root of all) which you have spoken as an act of kindness to me, my delusion has been dispelled. O Lotus-eyed, I have heard from you in detail an account of the origin and dissolution of beings and also your immortal glory. 1-2

Now what do you want?

O Lord Supreme, as You have declared Yourself, so You are—But I want to see Your divine form in whose limb infinite universes pervade. If You consider me capable of beholding it, show me your Eternal Self. 3-4

Śrī Bhagavān said—O Arjuna, behold not only one but hundreds and thousands of My multifarious divine forms, of diverse colours and different shapes. 5

What more should I behold, O Lord?

Behold the Ādityas, the Vasus, the Rudras, the Aśvinīkumāras and the Maruts and many marvellous forms never seen before. 6

O Lord, where should I behold all of them?

Behold, in this body of Mine, the entire creation

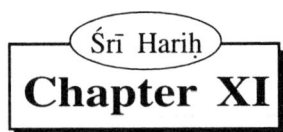

both animate and inanimate and also whatever else you desire to see.* 7

O Lord, You are asking me to behold the whole creation, but I can't behold anything. What should I do?

O brother, you can't see Me with these gross eyes of yours; therefore I bestow upon you divine eye. With this behold My Divine Power. 8

What did Lord Kṛṣṇa do after saying so, O Sañjaya?

Sañajya said—Having thus spoken, the great Lord of Yoga revealed to Arjuna His Supreme Divine Form. 9

What type of form did He reveal?

He revealed the form possessing many mouths and eyes, with many a wonderful sight, with many divine ornaments, wielding many uplifted divine weapons, wearing divine garlands and clothes, besmeared all over with divine sandal-pastes; all wonderful, infinite, having faces on all sides. 10-11

Why was his form all wonderful, O Sañjaya?

If the splendour of a thousand suns were to blaze forth all at once in the sky, even that would hardly be like the splendour of the Cosmic-Form. 12

Where did Arjuna behold that Form?

Arjuna behold in the person of that Supreme

---

* Arjuna wanted to know whether they would win or lose (2/6). So Lord Kṛṣṇa tells him that he should also see the result of the war in a limb of his body.

Deity, comprised in one limb, the whole universe with its manifold divisions. 13

What was the effect of that sight on Arjuna, O Sañjaya?

Arjuna, struck with amazement, his hair standing on end; bowing his head to the Divine Lord in adoration, with joined palms, spoke. 14

What did Arjuna speak, Sañjaya?

Arjuna said—O Lord, I behold in Your body all the gods and multitudes of different beings, Brahmā seated on his lotus-seat, Lord Śiva on Kailāsa, all Ṛṣis (Sages) and celestial serpents. 15

O Universal Form, O Lord of the universes, I behold You, infinite with forms on all sides with numerous arms, bellies, faces and eyes, I see neither Your beginning nor middle or end. I see You with diadem, club and discus (Cakra), a mass of splendour shining all around, hard to look at, all round dazzling like that of blazing fire and Sun and immeasurable on all sides. 16-17

O Lord, You are the Imperishable, the Supreme Being to be realized; You are the Ultimate Resort of this universe. You are the Imperishable Guardian of eternal Dharma (Duty and Righteousness) this is my conviction. 18

Is it your conviction only or do you also see, O Arjuna?

I see You without beginning, middle and end, infinite in power, with numberless arms, the Sun and the moon being Your eyes, the burning fire Your mouth and You are scorching this universe with your radiance. 19

O Noble Souled, the space between heaven and earth and all the quarters are filled by You alone. Seeing this marvellous, dreadful Form of Yours, the three worlds are trembling with fear. Those hosts of gods (whom I saw in heaven) are entering You; some out of fear with palms joined are chanting Your names and glories, bands of great Ṛṣis (Sages) and Siddhas (Perfected souls) by saying "May it be well!" May there be peace are extolling You with sublime hymns. 20-21

The Rudras, Ādityas, Vasus, Sādhyas, Viśvedevas, Aśvinīkumāras, Maruts, Manes, Gandharvas, Yakṣas, Asuras and Siddhas, all are gazing at You utterly amazed. 22

O Mighty-Armed, seeing this vast Form of Yours, with myriad mouths and eyes, with myriad bellies and feet and myriad terrible tusks, the worlds are terrified and so am I. 23

O Viṣṇu, seeing your Form touching the sky, effulgent, many coloured, with mouths wide open, possessing large shining eyes, I with my innerself frightened, find neither courage nor peace. Seeing Your faces with fearful tusks, resembling the raging fire at the time of universal destruction, I know not the four quarters, nor do I find peace. Therefore, O Lord of the gods and Abode of the universe, be kind to me. 24-25

With the principal warriors on our side, Bhīṣma, Droṇa and Karṇa also are entering You. Those sons of Dhṛtarāṣṭra with hosts of kings are rushing headlong into your fearful mouths set with terrible tusks, some are seen stuck up between your teeth with their heads crushed to powder. 26-27

As torrents of rivers rush towards the sea, so are those warriors of the mortal world entering Your blazing mouths. As moths rush with a great speed into the blazing fire for destruction, even so are all these people such as Duryodhana etc., out of delusion, very rapidly entering your mouths for their destruction and You with Your burning mouths are licking all those people on all sides. O Viṣṇu, Your terrible brilliance is burning the entire universe. 28—30

O Supreme Deity, I bow down to You, be kind. I wish to know You, the Primal Being, in essence. Tell me who You are so fierce in form?

Śrī Bhagavān said—I am the mighty Time the destroyer of the whole world.

Why have You come here, O Lord?

I have come here to destroy all these people.

Will anyone survive?

Even without you fighting all those warriors arrayed in the enemy's camp will not survive. They have already been slain by Me. Therefore you, arise and win glory; and conquer the enemies and enjoy the affluent kingdom.

Then why should I fight?

You should become a mere instrument. 31—33

But O Lord, how shall I get victory over brave warriors such as Bhīṣma, Droṇa, Jayadratha and Karṇa etc.?

Bhīṣma, Droṇa, Jayadratha, Karṇa and other brave warriors have already been killed by Me; fear not. Fight and you will surely conquer your enemies in the war. 34

What happened after this, Sañjaya?

Sañjaya said—Hearing these words of Lord Kṛṣṇa, Arjuna, trembling, bowed to Him with joined palms, and bowing again in extreme terror spoke to Lord Kṛṣṇa in a faltering voice. 35

Arjuna said—O immanent Lord, it is proper that the world is delighted and is filled with love by chanting Your names and glory; terrified Rākṣasas (demons) are fleeing in all directions and all the hosts of Siddhas (Perfected souls) are bowing to You. 36

Why is it proper, Arjuna?

O Lord, it is proper because You are Infinite, You are the Lord of the gods, You are the Base of the universe; You are the Imperishable. You are that which is existent (Sat), and that which is non-existent (Asat) and also that which is beyond both. O Great soul, You are the Progenitor of Brahmā himself and the Guide of the guides. So why should the hosts of perfected souls not bow to You? 37

You are the Prime Deity, the most Ancient Person; You are the supreme Resort of the universe. You are the knower and the knowable and the Supreme Abode. It is You who pervade the entire universe. 38

You are Vāyu (Wind-god), Yama (god of death), Agni (Fire-god), Varuṇa (the deity of waters), Prajāpati (the creator of the universe), Moon-god, and the father of Brahmā himself. Therefore, salutation, salutation to You, a thousand times and again and again salutation to You. Salutation to You from before and from behind and from all sides. You are infinite in might and immeasurable in strength. You pervade the entire universe and therefore You are all. 39-40

O Lord, ignorant of Your greatness and reality, thinking You only a friend, whatever I have rashly said from heedlessness or love addressing You as 'O Kṛṣṇa, O Yādava, O Friend and in whatever way I have insulted You in jest while playing, reposing in bed, sitting or dining either alone or in company of friends and family, I implore you to forgive me. 41-42

You are the father of the animate and inanimate creation, You are worthy of adoration, You are the greatest Teacher of teachers. O Possessor of incomparable glory, in all the three worlds there is no one else equal to You; who then can excel You? Therefore, O Lord bowing down, prostrating my body, I seek to propitiate You. It behoves You to condone my fault as a father condones the fault of his son, as a friend that of his friend and loving husband that of his beloved wife. 43-44

O.K. brother, what more do you want now?

I rejoice having seen Your wondrous form which was never seen before; at the same time my mind is tormented by fear. O Lord of the gods, O Abode of the universe, I pray to You to be pleased and reveal to me that Divine Form, the Form of Lord Viṣṇu with four arms, adorned with a diadem on the head and holding a mace, a discus, a conch and a lotus in Your hands. 45-46

Śrī Bhagavān said—O Arjuna, being pleased with you, I have shown you, by My power, this shining, primal and infinite Universal Form, which was not seen before by anyone else than you. 47

By what means can a man see Your Universal Form, O Lord?

By no means. O hero of the Kurus, neither by the study of the Vedas nor by rituals, nor by gifts, nor by sacrifices, nor by austere penances can this Form of Mine be seen in this mortal world by anyone else than you. 48

But O Lord, I am very much afraid by seeing this dreadful Form. What should I do?

O brother, be not afraid nor perturbed on seeing this dreadful Form of Mine. Now with a fearless and complacent mind behold once again the same Form of Mine. 49

O Sañjaya, what Form did Śrī Bhagavān reveal to Arjuna then?

Sañjaya said—Having thus spoken to Arjuna, Bhagavān Vāsudeva revealed to him His four-armed Form and then assuming his two-armed gentle form consoled Arjuna who was frightened. 50

You are no longer frightened Arjuna, are you?

Arjuna said—O Janārdana, (who is adored for fulfilment of desires) seeing this gentle human form of Yours, I have become composed and am restored to my normal self again. 51

Śrī Bhagavān said—This Form of Mine (with four-arms) which you have seen is very difficult to perceive. Even the gods are always eager to behold this Form. Neither by study of the Vedas, nor by penance, nor by charity nor by ritual can I be seen in this Form as you have seen Me. 52-53

How can You be seen then?

O Scorcher of foes, Arjuna, I can be seen in this form (with four-arms) through single-minded devotion. Not only seen but I can also be known in essence and be attained. 54

What is that single-minded devotion, O Lord?

O Pāṇḍava, to work for my sake, to be devoted to Me, to depend on Me, to have no attachment to the world and to be free from malice towards all beings is called the single-minded devotion. Such a devout devotee attains Me. 55

INTRODUCTION

Lord Kṛṣṇa in the thirty-third and the thirty-fourth verses of the fourth chapter explained the superiority of the path of knowledge (wisdom) and exhorted Arjuna to gain knowledge. Then He explained the glory of the knowledge. After that He explained the importance of the worship of the Supreme, Who is attributeless and formless in the sixteenth and the seventeenth verses and from the twenty-fourth to the twenty-sixth verses of the fifth chapter, from the twenty-fourth to the twenty-eighth verses of the sixth chapter and from the eleventh to the thirteenth verses of the eighth chapter.

In the forty-seventh verse of the sixth chapter He explained the glory of the devotee. From the seventh chapter to the eleventh chapter He time and again through the terms 'aham' (I) and 'mām' (Me) specially laid emphasis on the importance of the worship of God, Who is endowed with attributes and form and also is endowed with attributes but is formless. At last in the fifty-fourth and fifty-fifth verses of the eleventh chapter He glorified exclusive devotion and its fruit.

Śrī Hariḥ

Chapter XII

Arjuna said—As You have told now, many devotees, minds constantly fixed on You, adore You as possessed of form and attributes, and many adore Your Imperishable, Unmanifested form, of these two kinds of devotees who are better? 1

Śrī Bhagavān said—I consider those devotees to be the best who, endowed with supreme faith and ever steadfast, worship Me with mind centred on Me. 2

But what about those who adore Your unmanifested form?

Those, who, controlling all their senses and even-minded towards all, engaged in the welfare of all beings, constantly adore the Imperishable, the Indefinable, the unmanifest, the omnipresent, the unthinkable, the unchangeable, the Immovable, the Eternal, they too come to me. 3-4

Then how Your devotees happen to be the best?

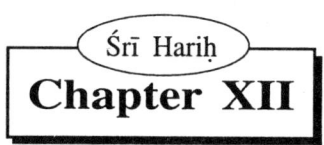

Greater is the difficulty of those whose minds are set on the unmanifested, for self-identification with the unmanifest is attained with difficulty by those who are centred in the body. But those who being solely devoted to Me, and surrendering all actions to Me, worship Me, constantly meditate on Me with single-minded devotion, O Pārtha, for such devotees whose minds are thus fixed on Me, I speedily become the deliverer from the ocean of birth and death. 5—7

How can I become such a devotee, O Lord?

Fix your mind on Me and establish your reasoning in Me alone. You will hereafter abide in Me alone. There is no doubt about it. If you can't steadily fix the mind on Me, then seek to attain Me through the Yoga (discipline) of practice. If you are unable even to take to practice, be intent on performing action for Me; you will attain perfection even by performing actions for My sake. If you are unable even to perform action for Me, then taking refuge in Me subduing your mind and senses, relinquish the fruit of all actions. 8—11

But according to You, is the last one, the renunciation of the fruit of actions, not an inferior means, O Lord?

No, brother, knowledge (of the scriptures) is better than practice without Yoga (equanimity); meditation is superior to knowledge without Yoga; and renunciation of the fruit of action is even superior to meditation without Yoga; for supreme peace immediately follows renunciation. 12

O Lord, what are the marks of anyone of the above mentioned four types of favourite devotees who have attained You, e.g., what are the qualities found in them?

He is free from malice towards all beings, not only this but he is friendly as well as compassionate. He has no feeling of 'I' and 'mine'; to him pleasure and pain are alike; he is forgiving by nature. He is ever content in all circumstances. His body, mind and senses remain under his control and his mind and intellect are surrendered to Me. Such a firm resolved devotee is dear to Me. 13-14

Who else is dear to You?

He by whom the world is not afflicted and whom the world can't afflict, he who is free from delight, envy, fear and anxiety is dear to Me. 15

O Lord, who else is dear to You?

He who craves for nothing, who is both internally and externally pure, is wise viz., he has achieved the aim (God-realization) for which human life was bestowed upon him, is unconcerned, has risen above all distractions and has renounced all undertakings which he does for pleasures and prosperity such a devotee is dear to Me. 16

Who else is dear to You?

He who neither rejoices in favourable situations nor hates unfavourable ones, nor grieves in unpleasant circumstances nor desires pleasant ones and who has renounced attachment and aversion to good and evil actions such a devotee is dear to Me. 17

Who else is dear to You?

He who is alike to friend and foe and likewise to honour and dishonour; who is the same in favourable and unfavourable situations, in pleasure and pain and is free from attachment to whom praise and reproach are equal, who is content with whatever comes unasked for, is without attachment to home and body, is steady minded—such a devotee* is dear to Me. 18-19

O Lord, You have told me that perfect devotees are dear to You. But who is extremely dear to You?

Those who endowed with faith and devotion are solely devoted to Me, and follow the marks of the perfect devotees as described above with interest—such striver devotees are extremely dear to Me. 20

* In this chapter there is the description of the marks of five types of perfect devotees. It means that different types of devotees possess different natures and their spiritual disciplines for God-realizations are different. But all of them possess two virtues in common. They are renunciation of affinity for the world and love (devotion) for God.

INTRODUCTION

At the beginning of the twelfth chapter Arjuna asked Lord Kṛṣṇa, "The devotees who, with their minds constantly fixed in You, adore You as possessed of form and attributes, and those who adore only the Imperishable, the Unmanifest—which of these two are better." The Lord responded, "I consider those the best, who endowed with supreme faith, having fixed their mind on Me, worship Me." Further He explained, "Those who adore only the Imperishable, the unmanifest also attain Me, but greater is their difficulty because they are centred in the body." Then He described the former type of worship in detail. Now He starts the thirteenth chapter in order to explain the latter kind of worship. First the Lord starts the topic of discrimination between Kṣetra (Body) and Kṣetrajña (Soul) (spirit).

Śrī Hariḥ

Chapter XIII

O Lord, those who are solely devoted to You endowed with attributes and form are extremely dear to You. But what about those who adore You as formless and attributeless?

Brother, they possess true knowledge (Discrimination).

O Lord, what is discrimination about?

It is about body and soul. This body is spoken of as the 'Field' (Kṣetra) and one who knows it (body) is called the knower of the Field (Kṣetrajña) by the wise. 1

What is the form of the knower of the field (Kṣetrajña)?

Know Me to be the Kṣetrajña in all the Kṣetras (bodies)*.

---

* The expression "Know Me to be Kṣetrajña in all Kṣetras" means that this body is a fragment of Prakṛti (Nature) and you are My fragment. Therefore have an inclination to Me and a disinclination for Prakṛti.

The second interpretation is that you have accepted your identification with Kṣetra (body) by mistake. But your identification with Me is axiomatic. So know this fact.

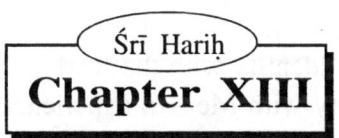

O Lord, what is that, knowing?

Kṣetra and Kṣetrajña are different; in my opinion to know this is real knowledge. It means that the Kṣetra has its identity with the world, while Kṣetrajña has his identity with Me—to experience this properly is knowledge in my opinion. 2

What are the different points which should be known for gaining knowledge of Kṣetra and Kṣetrajña?

There are six points which should be known. Four of them are about Kṣetra and two about Kṣetrajña. What that Kṣetra is, what it is like, what its evolutes are and whence is what, and also who that Kṣetrajña is and what his powers are—hear all this from Me in brief. 3

Where has this topic been described in detail, O Lord?

It has been described in detail by the seers and in different Vedic chants and also in the reasoned and decisive texts of the 'Brahmasūtras' separately. 4

What is that Kṣetra?

The five subtle elements (ether, air, fire, water and earth), the ego, the intellect, Primordial Matter, the ten senses, the mind and the five objects of sense (sound, touch, colour, taste and smell) these twenty-four constitute the Kṣetra.* 5

* Primordial Matter (Mūla Prakṛti) is the mother to all. She gave birth to intellect. Intellect gave birth to ego.

What are the evolutes of that Kṣetra?

Desire, aversion, pleasure, pain, the body, consciousness, and firmness—thus I have briefly described this Kṣetra with seven evolutes (modifications). 6

How should I acquire the knowledge of the Kṣetra, that it is different from Kṣetrajña?

1. Absence of pride 2. Freedom from hypocrisy 3. Non-violence with body, mind and speech 4. Forgiveness 5. Straight forwardness of body, mind and speech 6. Service of the preceptor (teacher) 7. Purity of the body and mind 8. Steadfastness in spiritual discipline 9. Self-control 10. Dispassion towards the objects of senses 11. Absence of egoism 12. Constant perception of pain and evil inherent in birth, death, old age and disease 13. Absence of attachment 14. Non-identification of self with son, wife, home etc. 15. Constant equanimity both in favourable and unfavourable circumstances. 16. Unflinching devotion to Me through exclusive attachment of mind to Me and indifference to the world. 17. Nature of living in secluded place.

Ego gave birth to five subtle elements—ether, air, fire, water and earth. These five elements gave birth to ten senses, a mind and five objects of sense—sound, touch, colour, taste and smell. But nothing originated from senses, mind and objects of senses. Therefore they are 'Vikṛti'. It means that the first seven are 'Prakṛti-Vikṛti' while the remaining sixteen are 'Vikṛtis'.

18. Distaste in the company of men. 19. Constant meditation on God's existence. 20. Observing God everywhere.

All this is declared knowledge, because by this knowledge the body will be perceived as 'this', and different from the 'self' and what is contrary to this is called ignorance, because with it one identifies the self with the body. 7—11

What is the essence which is acquired by the knowledge of Kṣetra and Kṣetrajña?

That is the knowable (Supreme Soul) God. I shall describe that knowable by knowing which one attains immortality.

What is the form of that knowable?

That is without beginning and end and He is the Supreme Brahma. He can neither be called 'Sat' (being) nor 'Asat' (non-being).* 12

How is He then?

With hands and feet everywhere, with eyes, head and face everywhere; with ears everywhere. He stands pervading all. Though devoid of all senses, He illumines all sense-objects. He is unattached but is the

---

* He can be called neither 'Sat' nor 'Asat', the reason is that without having the feeling of 'Asat', we can't use the word 'Sat' for the Supreme Soul. We also can't call him 'Asat', because the real (being) never ceases to be. So 'Sat' and 'Asat' do not apply to him. He is Pure Consciousness or Absolute Immortality.

sustainer of all. He is attributeless, but is the enjoyer of qualities (Guṇas). 13-14

How is this contradiction possible in him?

All the contradictions merge in him, because He is without, and within all beings and He constitutes both animate and inanimate creation viz., there is no existence except Him. He is farthest as well as nearest.* He is incomprehensible because of His subtlety viz., He is beyond the reach of sense and mind. So there is no contradiction in Him. 15

Why is there no contradiction in Him, O Lord?

Though indivisible yet He seems to be divided among beings—(things-). He is to be known as the creator, sustainer and destroyer viz., He Himself takes the form of creation, sustenance and destruction. He should be explored. 16

---

* Far and near can be in three ways—place, time and thing. As far as place is concerned, he is farthest as well as nearest. So far as time is concerned, He was in the past, He is at present and He will remain in future. As the things are concerned, He existed before the things came into existence, will remain when they are destroyed and He is now in the form of things.

This verse is the gist of this topic. If we understand this verse in the right perspective and meditate on its theme we come to know that God is everywhere, all the time, in all the things and then this feeling will remain with us automatically whether we are in solitude or in practical life.

What is His Form?

He is the light of all lights of senses, mind and intellect. He is the Illuminator of all knowledges. He is beyond darkness. He is knowledge, the object of knowledge and also worth attaining through knowledge. He is seated in the hearts of all.* 17

What else is to be known and what is the importance of that knowledge?

Kṣetra, knowledge and the knowable, all these three are to be known. The devotee, who knows the three properly, enters into My being viz., he realizes that he has identity with Me. 18

A devotee having known Kṣetra, knowledge and the knowable (object of knowledge) realizes his identity with You. But the striver who wants to follow only the discipline of knowledge (Jñāna), what knowledge is necessary for him?

It is necessary to know the Matter (Prakṛti) (Kṣetra) and spirit (Puruṣa) (Kṣetrajña) separately and correctly and the fact that both of them are without beginning.

When both are without beginning, from where do modifications and qualities (Guṇas) emanate?

All modifications and qualities (Guṇas) are born of Matter (Prakṛti). Moreover Prakrti is said to be the root of all activities, means (Karaṇa) and doership.

---

* In 13/13 there is the description of the Lord's Cosmic Form, while in this verse He is described as the light of all Lights viz., in Light-Form.

O Lord, in what aspect is spirit (Puruṣa) the cause?

Spirit is said to be the cause in the experience of pleasure and pain. 19-20

When does spirit become cause for experiencing pleasure and pain?

Spirit seated in Matter (Prakṛti), accepting the relationship with it experiences Guṇas (qualities) and attachment to these Guṇas is the cause of his birth in high and low wombs. 21

What are the characteristics of spirit?

Spirit, even when dwelling in this body is really transcendent and is the Supreme Soul. But because of its relationship with the body which is the effect of matter, it has been declared to be the 'Witness', because of approval the 'Guide', because of its support the 'Feeder', because of the experience of pleasure and pain the 'Experiencer' and because of accepting its lordship the 'Supreme Lord.' 22

O Lord, what accrues by having this knowledge of 'Spirit' (Puruṣa) and Matter (Prakṛti)?

He, who thus knows attributeless Puruṣa and Prakṛti with its threefold qualities, even though engaged in all sorts of activities approved by the Sacred books, is not born again viz., he is liberated from the cycle of birth and death. 23

Is there also any other means to know that Puruṣa?

Yes, there is. Some by meditation behold the Self

in their own heart, others behold (attain) by proceeding alongwith the path of knowledge and other again by treading the path of action. 24

Is there any easy means also?

Yes, those who don't know the spiritual means such as the Yogas of meditation and knowledge etc., but only obey the commands of liberated great souls also transcend death viz., are emancipated. 25

O Lord, how do they transcend death?

O best of the Bharata family, whatever beings, animate or inanimate are born, know them as emanated from the union of Kṣetra (Matter) and Kṣetrajña (Spirit). But those beings who don't accept relationship with Kṣetra transcend death and are liberated from the cycle of birth and death. 26

How should one be free from this union?

One should realize his axiomatic relationship with God & renounce relationship with Matter.

He, who sees the Supreme Lord as the only imperishable substance abiding equally in all perishable beings, beholds the reality and becomes free from this union. By seeing the same Lord dwelling equally in all, the striver does not accept his identity with the body. Then he does not kill himself by the self viz., he does not accept his death by the death of the body and therefore reaches the Supreme State. 27-28

Now how to renounce relationship with Matter (Prakṛti) (body)?

He, who sees that all actions are performed by Prakṛti alone, loses the sense of doership and when he perceives the bodies of beings as rooted in Prakṛti and emanating from Prakṛti, that very moment he attains Brahma and has no affinity for Prakṛti (Matter). 29-30

Why does it so happen?

O Son of Kuntī, because of being without beginning and without attributes, this spirit is nothing else than the imperishable Paramātmā (Supreme Soul). It dwelling in the body neither acts nor is tainted viz., it is neither a doer nor an experiencer. 31

How is it not contaminated (tainted)?

As the all-pervasive ether is not contaminated, by reason of its subtlety, so is the self seated everywhere in the body, not the least contaminated. 32

How does the spirit not act, O Lord?

As the; One Sun illumines the whole world but has no doership of illumination, so does this Kṣetrajña (spirit) without having doership illumines the whole Kṣetra (Field). In this way those, who perceive with the eye of wisdom this distinction between Kṣetra (Field) and Kṣetrajña (Knower of the Field) and see themselves separate from Prakṛti (Matter) and its evolutes, attain the Supreme Soul. 33-34

INTRODUCTION

At the end of the thirteenth chapter Lord Kṛṣṇa said that he, who with the eye of wisdom perceives the difference between Kṣetra and Kṣetrajña, attains the Supreme. Now the question arises what that wisdom (Jñāna) is, what its value or glory is and how it is gained. The Lord starts the fourteenth chapter in order to answer these questions. Connection with Prakṛti and its evolutes leads to bondage. The Lord in the thirteenth chapter explained how to renounce connection with Prakṛti. Now He starts the fourteenth chapter in order to explain the method of renouncing connection with its evolutes, the Guṇas. In the first two verse He glorifies wisdom.

Śrī Hariḥ

Chapter XIV

Śrī Bhagavān said—I shall impart to you once more the supreme wisdom (knowledge), the best of all wisdoms, by knowing which, all sages have attained the highest perfection. 1

What else is the importance of that wisdom, O Lord?

Those, having acquired this wisdom, have entered into My Being viz., have attained unity with Me; they are neither born at the time of new creation, nor are they tormented during final dissolution. 2

How do beings take birth at the time of new creation?

O Bhārata, My Prakṛti is the womb of all creatures in that I place the seed.* The birth of all beings follows from this combination. Therefore of all the bodies that take birth from different wombs, My Prakṛti is the conceiving mother and I am the seed giving father. 3-4

When You are the father of the entire creation how do beings get bound?

O mighty-armed, attachment to the Nature-born

---

* Placing the seed by 'God' means that at the beginning of the creation God according to the qualities, actions and nature of beings, enables them to have their relationship with Prakṛti.

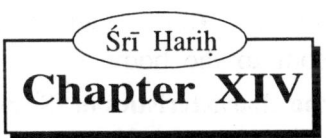

qualities of 'Sattva', 'Rajas' and 'Tamas' bind the imperishable soul to the body. 5

What are the characteristics of 'Sattva'? How does it bind the soul to the body?

O sinless Arjuna, Sattva, being stainless, is illuminating and flawless, but it binds the soul to the body by creating attachment to happiness and wisdom. 6

What are the characteristics of 'Rajas' and how does it bind?

O Son of Kuntī, Rajas is of the nature of passion, as born of thirst (cupidity) and attachment. It binds the soul to the body by attachment to action. 7

What are the characteristics of 'Tamas' and how does it bind?

O Arjuna, Tamas born of ignorance is the deluder of all embodies beings. It binds the soul to the body through heedlessness, indolence and sleep. 8

What do the three 'Guṇas' do before binding the soul, O Lord?

O Bhārata, Sattva dominates by binding one to happiness, Rajas by binding to action; while Tamas dominates, clouding wisdom binding one to heedlessness. 9

How does anyone of them dominate a being, O Lord?

O Arjuna, Sattva prevails suppressing Rajas and Tamas; Rajas prevails suppressing Sattva and Tamas; and Tamas prevails suppressing Sattva and Rajas. 10

What are the symptoms of the predominance of 'Sattva'?

When in this body, as well as in the mind and senses, the light of knowledge and wisdom beams, then 'Sattva' should be regarded as predominant. 11

What are the symptoms of the predominance of 'Rajas', O Lord?

When greed, activity, undertaking of actions with a selfish motive for pleasure and prosperity, restlessness and longing for enjoyment etc.,—these arise, then Rajas should be regarded as predominant. 12

What are the symptoms of the predominance of 'Tamas'?

O Kuntīnandana, when obtuseness, inactivity, carelessness and delusion—these arise, then Tamas is predominant. 13

What fate does a man meet with if he dies when those 'Guṇas' are predominant?

If a person dies when 'Sattva' is predominant, he gains the faultless (Pure) worlds. If he dies, when 'Rajas' is predominant, he is born among human beings while dying during the predominance of Tamas, he is born as an animal, a bird etc., and in the wombs of the inerts. 14-15

Why is it so?

It is so because they perform actions according to their 'Guṇas'. So the fruit of 'Sāttvika' action is pure (faultless) the fruit of Rajas is sorrow and the fruit of Tamas is ignorance (delusion). It means that such as the temperaments of goodness etc., bear fruit, so do the Sāttvika actions etc., bear fruit. 16

What is the cause of temperaments and actions?

These three Guṇas are the cause of temperaments and actions. Wisdom arises from Sattva; greed from Rajas; likewise heedlessness, stupor and ignorance arise from Tamas. 17

What type of fate do these men established in the three Guṇas meet with?

Those who are established in Sattva go to higher regions such as heaven etc., those of a Rājasika nature go to the region of men; while these of a Tāmasika temperament descend into the infernal regions (hells) etc. 18

Then who realizes You?

When the seer (wise) perceives no agent other than the Guṇas and knows himself beyond these Guṇas, he enters into My being. Having transcended the three Guṇas out of which the body is produced and freed from birth, death, old age and sorrow, he enjoys immortality. 19-20

Arjuna said—What are the marks of a person who has risen above the Guṇas?

Śrī Bhagavān said—O brother, to light which is born of Sattva, or activity which is born of Rajas, or delusion which is born of Tamas, he feels no aversion when they are present, and does not long for them when they are absent. He, sitting like a witness, is not moved by the Guṇas. He knowing that the Guṇas operate among the Guṇas, remains firmly established in the self and is never shaken.

What is the conduct of such a person who has risen above the Guṇas?

He is alike in pleasure and pain, having patience is established in the Self, regards a clod of earth, a stone and a piece of gold as equal in value; receives both pleasant and unpleasant things in the same spirit and views censure and praise alike. He remains the same in honour and dishonour, is equal to friend and foe and has renounced the sense of doership—he is said to have risen above the Guṇas.

What is the method to rise above these Guṇas?

He, who worships Me with an exclusive devotion transcending the three Guṇas becomes eligible for attaining Brahma. 21—26

When a devotee worships You, how can he become eligible for attaining Brahma?

O brother, he becomes eligible, for I am the abode (Base) of Brahma, of Immortality, of Eternal Virtue (Dharma) and of Absolute Bliss viz., I am called by these different names. 27

INTRODUCTION

In response to Arjuna's questions "Those devotees who ever earnest, worship Thee and those who worship the Imperishable and the Unmanifested—which of them are better versed in Yoga?" the Lord declared the former to be superior to the latter. In the fifth verse the Lord while comparing the two declared." The difficulty of those whose thoughts are set on the Unmanifested is greater, for the goal of the Unmanifested is hard to reach by the embodied beings. How to overcome this difficulty—this topic as well as the description of the Absolute has been given in the thirteenth and the forteenth chapters.

In the twenty-first verse of the fourteenth chapter Arjuna asked "What are the marks and conduct of him, who has transcended the three modes (Guṇas) and how does he transcend them?" In response to this the Lord described the marks and conduct of the person who has transcended the three modes in verses twenty-second to the twenty-fifth; while in the twenty-sixth verse He explained unswerving devotion as the means to transcend the three modes for the devotees, who worship God with attributes. It means that the devotee who has exclusive devotion to God (who totally depends upon Him) transcends the three modes easily. The expression 'avyabhicāreṇa bhaktiyogena' stands for freedom from dependence on the world through the 'path of devotion; the term 'Yaḥ' stands for the soul while the term 'mām' stands for God. So in the fifteenth chapter there is the description of these three subjects in detail.

Man (soul) being a fragment of God is transcendental but he is bound because of his identification with, attachment to and for the body (world) the evolute of the modes. He is not liberated from these modes so long as he does not know the Lord, Who has transcended the modes. Therefore the Lord introduces the fifteenth chapter in order to explain His glory and secret to enable a striver to cultivate unswerving devotion.

A man (soul) is a fragment of God (Gītā 15/7) and so he has his affinity only for God. But by error he assumes his affinity for the body, senses, mind and intellect, etc., which are evolutes of Nature only by regarding them as 'I' or 'mine'. This is the main stumbling block to exclusive devotion. In order to remove this stumbling block the Lord in the first five verses of the fifteenth chapter, having described the universe as a Pīpala tree, exhorts Arjuna to cut it down as under with the axe of dispassion.

Śri Hariḥ

Chapter XV

You are the Abode of Brahma, of Immortality etc. Then who is the abode of this world?

Śrī Bhagavān said—I am the abode of this tree in the form of the world too. This tree (the world) has its root above and branches below. It is called 'Aśvattha' (Pīpala tree) because it is not today as it was yesterday. It is called imperishable because its origin or its end is not known and it ever flows. The actions with their fruits mentioned in the Vedas are called its leaves. One who knows this tree in reality, is the knower of the Vedas. 1

What type of tree is it, O Lord?

The branches of this tree, nourished by the three Guṇas of Sattva, Raja and Tama, spread in the lower, middle and upper worlds. Five sense-objects of sound, touch, form, taste and smell are its buds (tender leaves). (Thinking of the sense-enjoyments is the sprouting forth of the new tender leaves.) But the root of the branches of this tree is this world of human beings, because the fruit of actions performed in this human life is reaped in all the worlds (births). 2

What are the characteristics of this tree?

Its nature, true and beautiful, as it seems, is actually not perceived on serious thought; because it has neither beginning, nor end nor even existence.

Then what should the man do to renounce this affinity?

The man cutting down this tree (world) with its branches of identification, attachment and desire etc., with the formidable weapon of dispassion, should seek the Supreme State (God).

What should he do if he can't seek the Supreme State, O Lord?

He should seek refuge in the Primal Person having reached whom, one never returns and from whom has emanated this beginningless flow of creation. 3-4

What happens if one seeks refuge in the Primal Person?

One who seeks refuge in the Primal Person becomes free from pride and delusion. By conquering the vice of attachment he becomes free from evils such as the sense of mine etc., and his desires completely disappear, he constantly dwells in God, and becoming free from the pairs of opposite known as pleasure and pain attain the Imperishable State. 5

How is that Imperishable State, O Lord?

Neither the Sun nor the Moon nor fire can illumine it and having reached which men do not return. That Imperishable State is My Supreme Abode. 6

Why do men not return?

The Ātmā (Spirit) (Soul) in the body is an eternal portion of Myself and therefore having reached Me it does not return. But it commits an error that it accepts the mind and the five senses, the evolutes of Prakṛti (Matter) as its own. 7

What happens when it accepts the mind and five senses as its own?

As the wind carries away odours from their sources, even so the Jīvātmā (embodied soul), accepting itself as the Lord of the body, snatching the mind and the senses from the body, which it casts off, migrates into the body which it acquires viz., it takes birth and dies again and again. 8

What does the Jīvātmā do there, O Lord?

This Jīvātmā (embodied soul), depending on the mind, through the five sense-organs—the ear, the eye, the skin, the tongue and the nose enjoys the sense-enjoyments of sound, form, touch, taste and smell having attachment. 9

What is the result of sense-enjoyments with attachment?

The Soul departing from the body or dwelling in the body or enjoying the objects of senses remains detached and unconnected. But the ignorant people who enjoy the objects of senses don't know this reality.

Then who knows it?

Those who possess the eye of wisdom know it in reality. 10

Whose eye of wisdom is open and whose is closed, O Lord?

Those striving Yogīs, who have purified their hearts viz., have attached importance to the Ever-Attained, are able to know the self dwelling in their hearts viz., their eye of wisdom is open. But those ignorant people who have not purified their hearts in spite of endeavours perceive Him not viz., their eye of wisdom is closed. 11

What is that Self?

That Self is I. The light which residing in the sun illumines the whole world and which exists in the moon as well as in the fire, know that to be My light. It means that 'I' in the form of light in the sun, the moon and fire illumines the whole universe.

O Lord, what other actions do You perform?

Entering the earth I sustain all beings by My power, and becoming the sapid moon, I nourish all herbs. 12-13

What other action do You perform?

Becoming the fire which dwells in the bodies of living beings and associated with the Prāṇa and Apāna breaths, I digest the four kinds of food (masticated, sucked, licked and swallowed). 14

O Lord, what is Your speciality?

I am installed in the hearts of all. Memory, wisdom and ratiocinative faculty etc., emanate from Me alone. It is I whom the four Vedas seek to know; I am the Author of the Vedānta as well as the Knower of the Vedas. 15

You are installed in the hearts of all. Who are they all?

In the world there are two kinds of Puruṣas (entities) perishable and imperishable; the bodies of all beings are perishable while the soul is imperishable.

Is there anyone else also distinct from these two?

Yes, the Supreme Person is distinct from both. He is called 'Paramātmā' (the Supreme Soul) and He sustains the three worlds and is designated as the imperishable Lord. 16-17

The Supreme Person is distinct. Then O Lord, who are You?

O brother, I am the Supreme Person. I am beyond the perishable Matter and superior to the imperishable soul. Therefore I am known in the world as well in the Veda as Puruṣottama (the Supreme Person). 18

What is the benefit a man derives by knowing You as 'Puruṣottama' (the Supreme Person), O Lord?

O Bhārata, undeluded devotee, who knows Me as the Supreme Person, knows all viz., nothing remains to be unattained by him. He worships Me with undivided devotion viz., he worships Me with his whole being. 19

Then why do all people not worship You with their whole being?

O Sinless Arjuna, this teaching imparted to you is most secret. By knowing this, nothing remains to be known, to be done and to be attained by My devotee. 20

INTRODUCTION

Lord Kṛṣṇa in the fifteenth verse of the seventh chapter explained in brief the traits of possessing the demoniac nature by declaring that those evil doers who are foolish and who have embraced the demoniac nature don't worship Him; while in the sixteenth verse He explained in brief those possessing the divine nature by declaring that those virtuous men worship Him. In the beginning of the eighth chapter Arjuna put seven questions based on the last two verses of the seventh chapter. The Lord answered those questions in whole of the eighth chapter.

The Lord at the beginning of the seventh chapter had promised that He would unfold to him the knowledge together with Realization. So He started the ninth chapter. In the twelfth verse of the ninth chapter He explains that the senseless persons with vain hopes, futile actions and fruitless knowledge embrace a nature which is demoniac, while in the thirteenth verse He declared that the great souls, who know Him as the prime cause of creation and worship Him constantly with undivided mind, possess a divine nature.

After the eleventh verse of the tenth chapter the Lord should have described the divine and demoniac natures in detail but Arjuna having been influenced by His grace offered praises to Him and prayed to Him to tell him His divine glories. While explaining His divine glories the Lord in the last verse of the tenth chapter declared, "What need is there O Arjuna, for the detailed knowledge? I stand supporting the whole universe with a single fragment of Myself." So Arjuna at the beginning of the eleventh chapter out of curiosity prayed to the Lord to reveal to him that cosmic form.

Having revealed to Arjuna His cosmic form, the Lord in the fifty-fourth and the fifty-fifth verses of the eleventh chapter explained the merits of exclusive devotion and the traits of such a devotee. So in the first verse of the twelfth chapter Arjuna inquired; "Which is considered to be more perfect; those who are properly engaged in Your devotional service or those who worship the Imperishable and the Unmanifested?" Therefore the Lord in the twelfth chapter described the devotees who are properly engaged in His devotional service and described the attributeless supreme Brahman in the thirteenth chapter and upto the twentieth verse of the fourteenth chapter. In the twenty-first verse of the fourteenth chapter Arjuna asked, "What are the marks of him who has risen above the three Guṇas (Modes)? What is his conduct? How does he transcend the three modes?" In response to his question the Lord explained exclusive devotion, the means to rise above the three modes i.e., He gave a hint of divine nature through exclusive devotion and of demoniac nature through adulterated devotion. He started the fifteenth chapter in order to explain how to develop exclusive devotion.

In the third verse of the fifteenth chapter there is mention of cutting down this tree with the weapon of detachment (i.e., renunciation of attachment) which is a mark of divine nature. In the fourth verse there is description of the divine nature in the expression, "I seek refuge in the Primal Person." It means that those who don't seek refuge in Him are of demoniac nature. In the nineteenth verse there is the description of divine nature when the Lord declares, "The undeluded person who thus knows Me as the Supreme Person, worships Me with his whole being." It means that those who don't worship Him are of demoniac nature.

Thus Lord Kṛṣṇa could not get an opportunity to explain in detail the divine and demoniac natures because Arjuna went on putting questions. Now He gets an opportunity to explain the divine and demoniac natures in detail. So He starts the topic.

Śrī Hariḥ

Chapter XVI

O Lord, who deserves this most secret teaching?

One who possesses divine traits.*

What are the marks of the person who possesses divine traits?

Śrī Bhagavān said—They are the following—

1. Fearlessness by depending on Me 2. Firm resolve of mind to attain Me 3. Equanimity in all circumstances in order to know Me in reality 4. Sāttvika form of charity 5. Control of the senses 6. Doing one's duty 7. To translate the principles of the sacred books into practice 8. Bearing of hardships for the sake of one's duty 9. Straightforwardness of body, mind and speech 10. Non-violence through body, mind and speech 11. Truthfulness and geniality of speech 12. Absence of anger even on provocation by regarding everyone as My manifestation 13. Renunciation of desire 14. Tranquillity of mind 15. Refraining from malicious gossip 16. Kindness to all creatures 17. Absence of attachment to the objects

---

* The term 'Deva' stands for Paramātmā (Supreme Soul). The traits which enable a devotee to attain the Lord are divine traits.

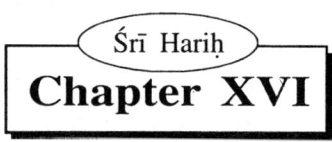

of senses even during their contact with the senses 18. Mildness of heart 19. Sense of shame in doing actions not sanctioned by the scriptures. 20. Absence of fickleness 21. Sublimity in body and speech 22. Forgiveness 23. Fortitude 24. External purity 25. Absence of malice 26. Absence of pride.

O Arjuna, these are the marks of the person who possesses divine traits viz., he who possesses these traits deserves My devotion.* 1—3

O Lord, who does not deserve Your devotion?

One who possesses demoniac traits.†

What are the marks of the person who possesses demoniac traits?

They are the following—

1. Hypocrisy 2. Arrogance 3. Pride 4. Anger

---

* In this context the question arises that those who possess the divine traits deserve devotion, but the vile sinner who does not possess these traits can't deserve it. It is a fact, but even if the vilest sinner worships God with exclusive devotion, he becomes a saint very quickly viz., he by God's grace possesses the divine traits quickly (Gītā 9/30-31).

† The term 'Asu' stands for life-breath. One who wants to delight in breath (life) and wants to maintain it, is called 'Asura'. Demons are those who by identifying themselves with bodies have a desire to live forever and enjoy pleasures. The traits which belong to dem[illegible] called demoniac traits.

5. Harshness in thought, word and deed 6. Ignorance (Non discrimination) O Son of Kuntī, one who possesses these traits does not deserve My devotion. 4

What is the outcome of the divine and demoniac traits, O Lord?

Divine traits are regarded as conducive to liberation while the demoniac nature as conducive to bondage. But O Pāṇḍava, you should not grieve, for you are born with divine virtues. 5

How is demoniacal nature conducive to bondage?

There are two types of men in this world—divine and demoniacal. The divine type has been described at length; hear from Me the demoniacal also. Men of demoniacal nature don't know what to do and what to refrain from. Hence they possess neither purity nor good conduct nor truth. 6-7

O Lord, why do they not possess purity etc.?

Their intellect is reverse. They say that the world is unreal and without a moral basis, Godless, born of mutual union of man and woman, brought about by lust; what else? 8

What kind of action do they perform?

Those men of atheistic outlook don't believe in their soul, their intellect is meagre; deeds are very fierce; they are enemies of the world. Such people apply their power for the destruction of others. Filled with insatiable desires, full of hypocrisy, pride and arrogance, holding evil ideas through delusion, they work in the world with impure resolve. 9-10

What is the concept of life for them?

Beset with immense cares ending only with death and given to the enjoyment of sensual pleasures and accumulation of wealth, they believe that, the highest limit of joy consists only in it. 11

What do they strive for, O Lord?

Held in bondage by hundreds of ties of expectation, given over to lust and anger, they strive to obtain, by unjust means, hoards of wealth for the enjoyment of sensual pleasures. 12

What are their expectations?

This wealth has been gained by me today and now I shall fulfil this desire. This wealth is, already mine and this wealth shall also be mine in future. This enemy has been already slain by us and others also shall we slay. We are lords, we are the enjoyers; we are perfect, powerful and happy. We are wealthy. There are so many people with us. Who else can be equal to us? We shall perform sacrifices, give charity and rejoice. Thus being deluded by ignorance they have many ambitions. 13—15

O Lord, what fate do they meet with after death?

Bewildered by many a fancy, enmeshed in the snare of delusion, addicted to the hoarding of wealth and enjoyment of sensual pleasures, they fall into the foulest hells. 16

What are the marks of those, demoniac in nature attached to pleasures which conduce them to ruin?

They are self-conceited, stubborn, filled with pride and intoxicated with wealth.

Can they not perform good actions, O Lord?

Yes, they perform good actions such as nominal sacrifice etc., for show and contrary to the scriptural ordinance. 17

Why do they do so?

They do so because they are given over to egoism, brute-force, pride, passion and anger.

What other feelings do they have?

They have malice; they find fault with Me and with others and they hate Me, who dwells in the bodies of others as well as in their own bodies. 18

What is the outcome of possessing this demoniacal disposition, O Lord?

These haters possessing cruel and evil nature, and vilest among men, I repeatedly throw into demoniacal wombs of animals such as dogs, donkeys, tigers, crows, owls, vultures, snakes and scorpions etc. 19

O Lord, then what happens to them?

O Son of Kuntī, cast into demoniac wombs, birth after birth, these deluded ones, without ever attaining Me, fall into still baser state viz., foulest of hells. 20

What is the root cause of their falling into hells, O Lord?

Passion (lust), anger and greed, these constitute the triple gate to hell leading to the damnation of the soul. Therefore one should abandon these three. 21

What happens after abandoning them?

O Kaunteya, the man released from these three gates to hell, works for his own salvation viz., does not indulge in forbidden actions, but performs actions approved by the scriptures without having any desire for their fruit and thus reaches the Highest-Goal. 22

Who fails to attain the Highest-Goal?

He, who casting aside the ordinance of the scriptures, acts according to his own sweet will, attains neither perfection (Purification of the inner sense), nor happiness nor the Supreme-Goal. 23

What is the criterion of good and evil actions?

Let the scriptures be the authority in determining what ought to be done and what ought not to be done. Therefore you should perform only such actions as are sanctioned by the ordinance of the scriptures. 24

INTRODUCTION

The Lord in the twenty-third verse of the sixteenth chapter declared that he, who having cast aside the ordinances of the scriptures, acts under the impulse of desire, attains neither perfection nor happiness nor the Supreme Goal. Listening to the Lord's statement Arjuna thinks that only a few people know those ordinances but they worship the gods etc., according to their caste, social order (Āśrama) and family tradition, impressions on mind etc. So Arjuna wants to know where such people stand. Therefore he puts the question to Lord Kṛṣṇa in the first verse.

Śrī Harih

Chapter XVII

Arjuna said—O Lord, what is the nature of the faith of those, who casting aside scriptural injunctions, perform sacrifice and worship with faith? Is it Sāttvika, Rājasika or Tāmasika? 1

Śrī Bhagavān said—The faith of men, born of their nature is of three kinds—Sāttvika, Rājasika and Tāmasika. 2

Why is it of three kinds?

O Bhārata, the faith of man is in accordance with his natural disposition. Faith constitutes the very being of man; therefore whatever the nature of his faith, that verily he is. 3

How to identify the nature of that faith?

Men of Sāttvika disposition worship the gods, those of Rājasika disposition worship Yakṣas (Genie) and Rākṣasas (Demons) while those of Tāmasika disposition worship spirits and ghosts. 4

How to identify those men who have no faith, O Lord?

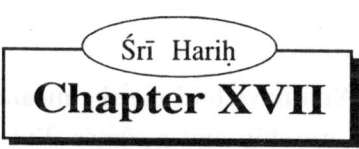

Those, lacking faith, practise austere penance not enjoined by the scriptures and are full of hypocrisy, egoism, desire and attachment. They torture the aggregate of elements that constitute their body and Me who dwell in their inner body. Know them to be of demoniacal resolve. 5-6

O Lord, You have told me the means to know the men by their worship and penance. But how to know the men who don't practise worship and penance etc.?

They can be known by the food they relish because the food also, which is dear to all (according to their nature), is of three kinds. So are sacrifice, penance and charity. Now hear their distinction. 7

Which foods are dear to the Sāttvika type of men?

Foods which promote longevity, purity, strength, health, joy and cheerfulness, which are savoury, oleaginous, nourishing and agreeable, are dear to the Sāttvika type of men. 8

Which foods are dear to the Rājasika type of men?

Foods which are bitter, sour, salted, very hot, pungent, dry, burning and giving rise to pain, grief and illness are dear tc the Rājasika type of men. 9

Which food is liked by the Tāmasika type of men?

Food which is half cooked, insipid, stinking (wine, onion, garlic etc.), stale, polluted and very impure (meat, fish, egg etc.), is liked by the Tāmasika type of men. 10

O Lord, You ordered me to hear three kinds of sacrifice, penance and charity?* Now tell me three kinds of sacrifice?

The sacrifice which is performed by men as a duty, enjoined by scriptural ordinance, having no desire for fruit, is the Sāttvika type of sacrifice. 11

What is Rājasika sacrifice?

The sacrifice which is offered in expectation of fruit or for selfish motive or for ostentation, know it to be Rājasika. 12

What is Tāmasika sacrifice?

The sacrifice which is without sanction of the scriptures in which no food distributed, no Mantras (Sacred formulas) are chanted and no fees are paid (to the officiating priest) and which is devoid of faith, is known as Tāmasika. 13

O Lord, how many kinds of austerity are there?

Austerity is of three kinds—of body, speech and mind. Worship of the Gods, of Brāhmaṇas (Priest class), of teachers and of the liberated souls, purity of the body by cleaning it with water, earth etc.,

* The Lord declared that the nature of a man's faith is identified by his worship and food. Such a man renounces the scriptural ordinance because of his ignorance. But how to identify the man who performs virtuous actions such as sacrifice etc., according to the scriptural ordinance? In order to explain it the Lord orders to hear three types of sacrifice, penance and charity.

uprightness, continence and non-violence—this is called austerity of the body. 14

What is austerity of speech?

Unoffensive, truthful, agreeable and beneficial speech and practice of the study of the sacred texts and constant repetition of the Divine Name—this is called austerity of speech. 15

What is austerity of mind?

Cheerfulness of mind, serenity, habit of meditation on God, self-control and purity of disposition—this is called austerity of mind. 16

If the threefold austerity is performed with supreme faith, by men having no desire for fruit, it is called Sāttvika. 17

What is Rājasika austerity, O Lord?

The austerity which is practised with the object of winning respect, honour and worship or for ostentation and is unstable and transitory in effect, is said to be Rājasika. 18

What is Tāmasika austerity?

The austerity done under a deluded understanding, with self-torture or with the object of causing injury to others, is said to be Tāmasika. 19

O Lord, now will You also tell the threefold gift (charity)?

The gift which is offered to one who can make no return, with the feeling that it is one's duty to give and which is given at the right place and time and to a worthy (deserving) person—that gift is held Sāttvika. 20

What is Rājasika gift?

The gift which is offered with a view to get some service in return or looking for its fruit or grudgingly, is said to be Rājasika. 21

What is Tāmasika gift?

The gift which is offered at an improper place and time to undeserving persons in a disrespectful and insulting manner, is said to be Tāmasika. 22

O Lord, how should a man having faith begin activities such as sacrifice, austerity and gift etc., which are sanctioned by the scriptures?

'Oṁ, Tat, Sat' this has been declared to be the threefold designation of the Supreme Soul. At the beginning of the creation the Brāhmaṇas, the Vedas and sacrifices were created by Him. Therefore such activities as sacrifice etc., should be begun by remembering the name of the Supreme Soul. 23

O Lord, where is 'Oṁ' uttered?

Acts of sacrifice, gift and austerity as enjoined by the scriptures are always commenced with the utterance of the word 'Oṁ' by those who believe in Vedic principles. 24

Where is 'Tat' used, O Lord?

With the idea that everything is for the Supreme

Soul called 'Tat' various kinds of sacrifice, penance (austerity) and gift are performed by the seekers of liberation without desiring any fruit in return. 25

Where is the term 'Sat' used?

O Pārtha, the Divine Name 'Sat' is used in the sense of truth and goodness, and it is also used in the sense of praiseworthy act. Steadfastness (faith) in sacrifice, austerity and gift is also designated as 'Sat'. Not only this but every action performed for the sake of the Lord is called 'Sat'. 26-27

O Lord, which actions are called 'Asat' (non-existent)?

O Pārtha, whatever sacrifice (oblation offered to the fire-god), gift offered and austerity performed as well as any other act, which are performed without faith are called 'Asat'. They are of no account either here (in the earthly life) or hereafter (after death) viz., they can't bear 'Sat' fruit anywhere. 28

INTRODUCTION

The Lord in the thirty-ninth verse of the second chapter described Sāṅkhyayoga (The Discipline of Knowledge) and Karmayoga (The Discipline of Action). These two disciplines were also mentioned in the third verse of the third chapter. Arjuna wanted to know these two paths (Disciplines). But as Lord Kṛṣṇa could not get an opportunity to explain the divine nature and the demoniac nature from the seventh chapter to the fifteenth chapter, similarly Arjuna could not express his curiosity from the third chapter to the seventeenth chapter.

Having mentioned the two paths in the third verse of the third chapter Lord Kṛṣṇa in the first verse of the fourth chapter explained that He taught the imperishable Yoga to the sun-god. Arjuna asked Him how he could believe that He taught the Yoga to the sun-god, because His birth was later while the birth of the sun-god was earlier. The Lord in response to his question talked of His divine births (incarnations) and divine actions. In the thirty-fourth verse of the fourth chapter He ordered him to gain that knowledge from the men of wisdom by prostration, by question and by service to them. Again in the forty-second verse of the fourth chapter He ordered him to establish himself in Yoga viz., Karmayoga (in the form of even-mindedness). So Arjuna at the beginning of the fifth chapter asked Lord Kṛṣṇa which of the two, the path of knowledge or the path of action (Karmayoga) was decidedly better for him. The Lord answered his question in the fifth chapter and started the sixth chapter of his own accord.

In the thirty-third and the thirty-fourth verses of the sixth chapter Arjuna put a question on the restlessness (fickleness) of mind. The Lord answered his question in brief. Arjuna from the thirty-seventh to the thirty-ninth verses put the question, "What fate does the striver, whose mind wanders away from Yoga (at the time of death) failing to attain perfection in Yoga, meet with?" The Lord answered the question in the sixth chapter. In the last verse of the sixth chapter the Lord declared his devotee the most devout among all the Yogīs. The Lord started the same topic in the seventh chapter where he described devotion in particular.

Lord Kṛṣṇa at the end of the seventh chapter while describing His entire form used the terms Brahma and Adhyātma etc. So at the beginning of the eighth chapter Arjuna put seven questions for the clarification of those terms. The Lord answered the first six questions in brief while He explained the seventh question in detail. Then He described the topic which was left in the seventh chapter, in the ninth chapter and upto the eleventh verse of the tenth chapter. Arjuna was very much pleased when he heard in the ninth, tenth and eleventh verses of the tenth chapter, of the devotees and the Lord's compassion to them. So Arjuna from the twelfth to the eighteenth verses praised Him and prayed to Him to tell him in detail His power of Yoga and His glories. Having described His important glories at the end of the tenth chapter He declares, "What need is there, O Arjuna, for the detailed knowledge? I stand supporting the whole universe with a single fragment of Myself." Hearing these words Arjuna prayed to Him to reveal to him His cosmic form. Having revealed His cosmic form the Lord declared that by unswerving devotion He can be seen and known and even entered into.

At the end of the eleventh chapter the Lord explained the merits of devotion and before that also He explained the merits of the worship of His absolute aspect (4/34—37; 5/13—26; 6/24—28 and 8/11—13); So Arjuna at the beginning of twelfth chapter asked, "The devotees who with their minds constantly fixed in You adore You and again those who worship the Imperishable and the Unmanifested—of these two who are better versed in Yoga!" In response to his question Lord Kṛṣṇa explained devotion and devotees in the twelfth chapter, while worship of the Imperishable and the Unmanifested in the thirteenth and the fourteenth chapter. In the twenty-first verse of the fourteenth chapter Arjuna asked, "What are the marks of him who has transcended the three modes of nature? What is his conduct and how does he get beyond the three modes?" So the Lord explained the marks and conduct of such a transcendental person and also explained exclusive devotion as the means to attain that state. The Lord started the fifteenth chapter in connection with His exclusive devotion. At the end of the chapter He declared that a person who knows Him as the Supreme Person worships Him with his whole being (heart spirit). He means to say that the persons of divine nature worship Him. It connotes that the persons of demoniac nature don't worship Him. Before this chapter also in the fifteenth verse of the seventh chapter and in the twelfth verse of the ninth chapter the demoniac nature, while in the thirteenth verse of the ninth chapter the divine nature have been described in brief. So the Lord started the sixteenth chapter in order to explain the divine nature and the demoniac nature.

Arjuna put the question at the beginning of the seventeenth chapter on faith which was in connection with the Lord's declaration which he made in the last but one verse of the sixteenth chapter. The Lord answered his question by describing the faith of three kinds in the seventeenth chapter. Now Arjuna expresses his desire to know the two paths of knowledge and of action, which were mentioned by Him in the third verse of the third chapter.

Śrī Hariḥ

Chapter XVIII

Arjuna said—O mighty-armed, O slayer of Keśī! I desire to know separately the true nature of Saṁnyāsa (Sāṅkhyayoga) and of Tyāga (Karmayoga). 1

Śrī Bhagvān said—There are four opinions of the men of wisdom about 'Saṁnyāsa' and 'Tyāga'.

O Lord, what are those opinions?

1. Some men of wisdom understand 'Saṁnyāsa' as the renunciation of actions, which are prompted by desire, 2. Other wisemen define 'Tyāga' as the abandonment of the fruits of all actions, 3. Some sages declare that all actions should be relinquished as evil, while 4. Others say that acts of sacrifice, gift and austerity should not be renounced. 2-3

O Lord, these are the opinions of the men of wisdom. But what is Your views in this respect?

O noble Arjuna, out of the two, Saṁnyāsa and Tyāga, hear from Me, the truth about this abandonment (Tyāga). Abandonment has been declared to be of three kinds. Acts of sacrifice, gift and penance should not be relinquished, but must be performed, for each of them is purifying to the wise. 4-5

Should only these noble acts be performed?

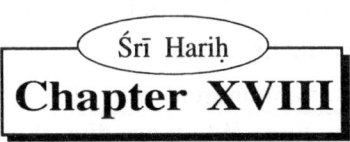

My considered and best opinion is that these acts of sacrifice, gift and penance and all other actions, which are approved by the scriptures, must be performed relinquishing attachment and fruit. 6

O Lord, abandonment has been described of three kinds by You. What are the characteristics of that abandonment?

Renunciation of action prescribed by the scriptures (Niyatakarma)* is not proper for anyone. Its abandonment out of ignorance has been declared as 'Tāmasika' form of abandonment. 7

What are the characteristics of Rājasika abandonment?

He, who forsakes his duty from fear of bodily discomfort because it is labourious, practises Rājasika form of abandonment. Such a person does not get the fruit of relinquishment viz., does not get peace. 8

What are the characteristics of Sāttvika abandonment?

O Arjuna, an action enjoined by the scriptures, which is performed as a duty, giving up

* There is some difference between 'Vihita Karma' and 'Niyata Karma'. All the actions approved by the scriptures are 'Vihita Karma'. For example there are so many fasts which should be observed according to the scriptures. But if a man observes all of them, when will he have a meal? It means that all 'Vihita Karmas' are not applicable to every person, out of these 'Vihita Karmas' he should discharge his obligatory duty according to his Varṇa (caste) pertaining to his livelihood and maintenance of the body. This duty is called 'Niyata Karma'.

attachment and fruit, is regarded as Sāttvika form of abandonment. 9

How can it be known that a striver has true renunciation?

The relinquisher relinquishes actions for fruit, also forbidden actions but he neither hates a disagreeable action nor is attached to an agreeable one. He imbued with the quality of goodness, free from doubt, remains established in the self. 10

Why should a man not get rid of complications by renouncing actions instead of performing them in a detached way?

Since it is not possible for an embodied being to renounce actions completely, it is said that he, who renounces the fruit of actions, has truly renounced. 11

What are the kinds of the fruit of action, O Lord?

Good, evil and mixed—threefold is the fruit of action e.g., agreeable conditions, disagreeable conditions and a mixture of both respectively hereafter for those who have not renounced the fruit; but there is none for those who have renounced the fruit.

What are the cause in the accomplishment of actions?

O Mighty-armed, in the accomplishment of all actions, five causes have been mentioned in the Sāṅkhya system, know them from Me. 12-13

Which are those five causes, O Lord?

The body, the agent (the self) (the Jīvātmā), the various organs, divergent activities of various kinds and destiny—are the five causes. Whatever action a man performs with his body, speech or mind, be it right or wrong—these five are its causes. 14-15

What do You mean by saying that in the accomplishment of actions there are five causes?

Actually the Ātmā (Spirit) is not the doer. All actions are performed with the body, mind and speech. But he who views the self as the doer is a man of imperfect understanding owing to his impure intellect. 16

What is the utility in viewing the Ātmā (the self) as the non-doer, O Lord?

He, whose mind is free fom the notion of doership and whose reason is not affected by the fruit of action, even though he may kill the people, he does not kill, nor is he bound by sin. 17

When the soul (Ātmā) has no connection with actions, what are the incentives to action?

Knowledge, the object of knowledge and knower—these form the threefold incentives to action; and the instrument, the action and the doer are the threefold constituents of action. 18

Which are more important—the incentives to action or the constituents of action? What is their classification?

Knowledge, action and doer are declared in the science of Guṇas to be of three kinds, according to the distinction of Guṇas (qualities). Hear them duly from Me. 19

Out of the three kinds what is Sāttvika knowledge?

The knowledge by which a striver sees one imperishable entity in all beings, undivided among the divided, is called Sāttvika. 20

What is Rājasika knowledge, O Lord?

The knowledge by which one sees the manifold existence of various kinds in all beings as separate, is known Rājasika. 21

What is Tāmasika knowledge?

The knowledge which clings to one individual (body) as if it were the whole, which is without reason, without any real object, and trivial, is declared as Tāmasika. 22

Out of the three kinds of action, which one is Sāttvika?

The action which is performed without the sense of doership, without passion or prejudice by one not desirous of the fruit, is said to be Sāttvika. 23

Which is Rājasika action?

The action which is performed by one craving for desire or with egoism or with much effort, is to be Rājasika. 24

What is Tāmasika action?

The action which is undertaken from delusion, without considering the result, loss, injury and one's own capacity, is declared to be Tāmasika. 25

O Lord, who is a Sāttvika agent (doer)?

The doer who is free from attachment, non-egoistic; endowed with firmness and vigour and unaffected by success or failure is called Sāttvika. 26

Who is a Rājasika doer?

The doer who is passionate, desires the fruit of action, is greedy, is given to violence and impure conduct and is affected by joy and sorrow, is declared to be Rājasika. 27

Who is a Tāmasika doer?

Unsteady, vulgar, stubborn, deceitful, malicious, slothful, despondent and procrastinating—such a doer is said to be Tāmasika. 28

You have described knowledge, action and doer—each of three kinds. Besides them what are other divisions, O Lord?

There are also divisions of reason (intellect) and firmness and it is very necessary to know them. Therefore hear the threefold division of reason and firmness, which is being told by Me in full. The intellect (reason) which duly knows—right action and wrong action, what must be done and what must not be done, fear and fearlessness, bondage and liberation, is Sāttvika. 29-30

What is Rājasika reason?

The reason by which one does not understand correctly what is right and what is wrong, or what ought to be done and what ought not to be done, is Rājasika. 31

What is Tāmasika reason?

O Son of Kuntī, the reason which, enveloped in ignorance, thinks the wrong (unrighteous) to be right (righteous) and regards all things contrary is Tāmasika. 32

O Lord, which is Sāttvika firmness?

O Pārtha, unswerving firmness by which through the Yoga (equanimity) one controls the activities of the mind, life-breaths and senses, is Sāttvika. 33

Which is Rājasika firmness?

The firmness, by which one holds fast to Dharma (Virtue), Artha (Prosperity) and Kāma (Desire), desirous of the fruit of each from attachment, is Rājasika. 34

Which is Tāmasika firmness?

The firmness by which a stupid person does not give up sleep, fear, grief, despondency and arrogance, is called Tāmasika. 35

Why does a man of Tāmasika disposition not give up sleep etc.?

He derives happiness out of them.

What is that happiness?

O Arjuna, now hear from Me three kinds of happiness (joy). That in which one finds enjoyment only through practice (of meditation worship) and whereby one reaches the end of sorrow; that which appear like poison in the beginning, but tastes as nectar in the end, born of the translucence of intellect due to Self-realization, is said to be Sāttvika. 36-37

What is Rājasika joy?

The joy, which is derived from the contact of the senses with their objects, though appear like nectar in the beginning, proves to be like poison in the end, is said to be Rājasika. 38

What is Tāmasika joy?

The joy which deludes the self (soul) both at the beginning and at the end, and which is derived from sleep, indolence and heedlessness is said to be Tāmasika. 39

O Lord, where else are these three Guṇas found?

O brother there is no existence anywhere on the earth, in heaven or among gods which is free from these three Guṇas (modes) born of Nature. 40

O Lord, what is the means to be free from these Guṇas?

O scorcher of foes, the duties of Brāhmaṇas, Kṣatriyas, Vaiśyas and Śūdras are divided according to the Guṇas born of their respective natures. Therefore, performing one's duty according to one's Varṇa (caste) is the means to be free from these Guṇas. 41

What are the duties of a Brāhmaṇa (Priest class)?

1. Control of mind 2. Control of senses 3. Undergoing hardships for the sake of duty 4. External and internal purity 5. Forgiveness 6. Uprightness of body and mind etc. 7. Knowledge of the Vedas and scriptures 8. Realization 9. Belief in God and the scriptures—these are Brāhmaṇa's inherent duties. 42

What are the duties of a Kṣatriya?

1. Heroism 2. Vigour 3. Firmness 4. Resourcefulness 5. Not fleeing from battle 6. Generosity (charity) 7. Rulership—these are the Kṣatriya's duty, born of his own nature. 43

What are the duties of Vaiśya?

1. Agriculture 2. Rearing of cows 3. Trade—these are the natural duties of Vaiśyas.

What are the duties of a Śūdra?

Service of all the three castes is the duty of a Śūdra, born of his own nature. 44

O Lord, what happens by discharging the duty born of one's nature?

Devoted to one's own duty without the desire for its fruit, one attains the highest perfection in the form of God-realization. Now listen how one realizes Him. 45

O Lord, how?

He from whom is the emanation of all beings and by whom the whole world is pervaded, by worshipping Him through the performance of his own duty, man attains perfection viz., realizes Him. 46

Why should a man perform his own duty only, O Lord?

O brother, better is one's own duty, though devoid of merit, than the duty of another well performed; because by performing one's own duty approved by the scriptures, one does not incur sin.

Therefore one should not abandon one's duty even though devoid of merit, because all undertakings are enveloped by some blemish just as fire is clouded by smoke. 47-48

Is there any method by which the duty may be free from blemish?

Yes, the method is Sāṅkhyayoga (The Discipline of Knowledge). Whose intellect is unattached everywhere, who has subdued his self and whose thirst for enjoyment has completely disappeared; such a person through Sāṅkhyayoga reaches the highest perfection of actionlessness i.e., his actions turn into inaction and he becomes totally free from blemish. 49

What is the order to attain the highest perfection of actionlessness?

Know from Me briefly the order how reaching such perfection in the shape of purity of heart one attains Brahma, the Absolute, who is the supreme consummation of knowledge. The person endowed with pure reason, restraining the self with firmness, renouncing the objects of senses, abandoning attractions and aversion, dwelling in a sacred and lonely place, eating light food; subduing speech, body and mind; always in meditation; endowed with dispassion; having abandoned egoism, violence, arrogance, desire, anger, greed; destitute of the feeling of mineness; and being calm becomes qualified to attain Brahma (the Eternal). 50—53

What happens when a person is qualified to attain Brahma (the Eternal)?

Such a devotee becoming one with Brahma, always remaining cheerful, neither grieves nor desires and becomes the same to all beings and thus attains surpeme devotion to Me. 54

What is the result of supreme devotion?

Through devotion he comes to know Me in reality, what I am and who I am; and thereby knowing Me in reality (essence), he forthwith enters into Me. 55

O Lord, is there any other method also to attain You?

Yes, there is a very good method.

What is that, O Lord?

One who with exclusive devotion takes refuge in Me alone that devotee ever performing all actions, by My grace attains the eternal imperishable state. 56

O Lord, what should I do?

O brother, having surrendered all actions to Me depend on Me alone viz., remove your attachment from all actions, depend on Me alone viz., remove your attachment from all actions and things etc., and resorting to equanimity, have your mind constantly fixed on Me. 57

What will happen when I fix my mind constantly on You?

By fixing your mind, you will by my grace,

overcome all obstacles. But if out of pride you don't listen to me, you will fall. 58

How shall I fall?

Prompted by egoism, you think that you will not fight, this determination of yours is vain; because your nature (of a Kṣatriya) will compel you to fight. O son of Kuntī, it is out of delusion, you don't want to fight. But bound by your own duty born of your nature, you will fight helplessly against your will because you are a Kṣatriya. 59-60

O Lord, how will the nature force me to fight?

O Arjuna, the Lord dwells in the hearts of all beings and He by His illusive power causes all beings to revolve according to their nature as though mounted on a machine. 61

So what should I do, so that I may not revolve as though mounted on a machine?

O Arjuna, seek refuge in God alone with exclusive devotion. By His grace you will become totally indifferent to the world and gain imperishable Supreme State. Thus I have imparted to you this knowledge of surrendering yourself to Him, which is more secret than secrecy itself. Reflect upon it fully and then act as you like. 62-63

O Lord, I don't want to do anything according to my will. Tell me what I should do?

Listen again to my supreme word, the most secret of all. You are very dear to me; therefore I shall tell you what is for your good. 64

What is good for me, O Lord?

Be devoted to Me, fix your find on Me, worship Me and bow to Me. By doing so you shall without doubt reach Me. This I truly promise to you; for you are very dear to Me. 65

What should I do if I am unable to do so?

Surrendering all duties to me seek refuge in Me alone. I shall liberate you from all sins, grieve not. 66

O Lord, this message is very easy and beneficial. May I convey this message to all the people?

No, no brother this supreme secret teaching should never be imparted to a man who is intolerant nor to him who is without devotion, nor to him who is unwilling to hear, nor to him who finds fault with Me. 67

Excluding this supreme word, whom should I impart the other teachings of the Gītā?

It should be imparted to my devotees. He, who with supreme devotion to Me, shall impart this most secret teaching of the Gītā to my devotees, shall attain me without any doubt. Not only this but among men there will be none to render Me a more loving service than he; nor shall anyone be dearer to Me than he, on the earth. 68-69

O Lord, if a person is unable to render such a service, what should he do?

He should study this sacred dialogue of ours. By

him I shall be worshipped by the sacrifice of wisdom; such is my conviction. 70

O Lord, what course should a man adopt if he is unable even to study the sacred dialogue?

The man who listens to this sacred dialogue of ours full of faith and an uncarping spirit, shall gain the higher worlds of the Virtuous. 71

O Pārtha, now I want to ask you whether you have heard this message with an attentive mind and whether your delusion, born of ignorance, has been destroyed. 72

Arjuna said—O Acyuta (one who doesn't deviate from His divine nature), my delusion is destroyed and I have regained memory (knowledge) by your grace, not by my efforts of listening to the message. I stand free from doubts and I shall obey You. 73

Sañjaya said—O King, thus I listened to this thrilling dialogue between Lord Kṛṣṇa and high souled Arjuna. 74

O Sañjaya, how did you get an opportunity to listen to his dialogue?

I heard this most secret dialogue direct from Lord Kṛṣṇa through the grace of Vyāsa, rather than in succession. 75

O Sañjaya, what is its effect on you?

O King, remembering again and again this holy and marvellous dialogue between Lord Kṛṣṇa and Arjuna, I am delighted again and again. 76

O Sañjaya, what else is the reason of your delight?

O King, by recalling that most marvellous cosmic form of Lord Kṛṣṇa, great is my astonishment and I rejoice again and again. 77

O Sañjaya, what conclusion have you drawn from all this?

Wherever is Lord Kṛṣṇa, the lord of Yoga and wherever is Arjuna, the wielder of the Gāṇḍīva bow, there are prosperity, victory, glory and righteousness—this is my conviction. 78

Note : *After the study of, "Gītā the Melody Eternal" (Gītā Mādhurya), the readers are requested to go through 'Sādhaka-Sañjīvanī' published by Gita Press which contains more details and which will enable them to have a proper understanding of the Gītā.*

Our English Publications

457 **Śrīmad Bhagavadgītā—Tattva-Vivecanī** With Sanskrit text, English Translation and Detailed Commentary (By Jayadayal Goyandka)

1080, 1081 **Śrīmad Bhagavadgītā—Sādhaka-Sañjīvanī** With Sanskrit Text, Roman Transliteration, English Translation and Detailed Commentary (By Swami Ramsukhdas) Set of two volumes

455 **Śrīmad Bhagavadgītā** (Sanskrit Text and English Translation) Pocket Size

534 **Śrīmad Bhagavadgītā** (Sanskrit Text and English Translation) (Hard Bound Edition) Pocket Size

1223 **Śrīmad Bhagavadgītā—Roman Gītā** (Sanskrit Text, Transliteration and English Translation) (Unbound)

452, 453 **Śrīmad Vālmīki-Rāmāyaṇa** (With Sanskrit Text and English Translation) Set of two volumes

1318 **Śrī Rāmacaritamānasa** (With Hindi Text, Roman Transliteration and English Translation)

786 **Śrī Rāmacaritamānasa** Medium Size

564, 565 **Śrīmad Bhāgavata** (With Sanskrit Text and English Translation) Set of two volumes

783 **Abortion Right or Wrong You Decide?** (By Gopi Nath Agrawal)

824 **Songs From Bhartṛhari**

494 **The Immanence of God** (By Madan Mohan Malaviya)

808 **Nava Durga** (Story with the Picture)

BY JAYADAYAL GOYANDKA

477 Gems of Truth [Vol. I]
478 Gems of Truth [Vol. II]
479 Sure Steps to God-Realization
481 Way to Divine Bliss
482 What is Dharma? What is God?
480 Instructive Eleven Stories
520 Secret of Jñānayoga
521 Secret of Premayoga
522 Secret of Karmayoga
523 Secret of Bhaktiyoga
694 Dialogue with the Lord During Meditation
1125 Five Divine Abodes
658 Secrets of Gītā
1013 Gems of Satsaṅga

BY HANUMAN PRASAD PODDAR

484 Look Beyond the Veil
622 How to Attain Eternal Happiness?
483 Turn to God
485 Path to Divinity
847 Gopīs' Love for Śrī Kṛṣṇa
620 The Divine Name and Its Practice
486 Wavelets of Bliss & the Divine Message

BY SWAMI RAMSUKHDAS

619 Ease in God-Realization
471 Benedictory Discourses
473 Art of Living
487 Gītā Mādhurya
472 How to Lead A Household Life
570 Let us Know the Truth
638 Sahaja Sādhanā
1413 All is God
621 Invaluable Advice
497 Truthfulness of Life
669 The Divine Name
552 Way to Attain the Supreme Bliss
562 Ancient Idealism for Modernday Living
1101 The Drops of Nectar (Amṛta Bindu)